Christopher Bursk

SELECTED POEMS

FUTURECYCLE PRESS

www.futurecycle.org

Published by FutureCycle Press
Lexington, Kentucky, USA

ISBN 978-1-938853-51-7

to the valiant George Drew, Herb and Pam Perkins-Frederick,
Ray Reilly, Helen Lawton Wilson,
and Duncan Sylvester

&

to my beloved Sadie, Maggie, Tyler, Josie, Zack, and Jake, Nora
and Gary, Christian and Christine, Justin and Danielle,
and Mary Ann

&

to my first heroes Edward Collins Bursk Jr. and John Howard Bursk

Contents

From
MAKING WINGS
PLACE OF RESIDENCE
LITTLE HARBOR

From
STANDING WATCH

Acknowledgments

Selected Poems

1

You've published enough books, old man.
Let someone else have a turn.
The letter doesn't say that, but it might as well
tell him that he's also exceeded his limit
of walks with his dog
or pick-up basketball games with his granddaughter
or afternoons saving the world
with the help of his grandsons and their plastic dolphins.

2

Please forgive my verbs for working so hard.
Hard work is all they've ever known.
Maybe not the best cover letter for an old man
to submit to the young editors at university presses.

3

It's raining. It's often raining when I write.
The drops throw themselves against the window.
They want to be in the poem too.
They don't care what it's about.

4

What are you writing about?
asks my four-year-old granddaughter.
She expects I've put her in yet another poem
and she wants out. Now.

5

I'm sorry, my wife says
when I open the letter that says exactly
what I was afraid it would.
It's the same voice she uses
when she cups her hand around a moth
and walks it to the door.
It darts off. It has important business to attend to
somewhere else.

6

How do others do it: sit at their desks
and labor over poems

in the hope that maybe a magazine named after a flower
or a constellation might get interested
in the day their mother forgot them at the rest-stop
or their cat decided to stop eating forever
or they fell in love with the color yellow
or looked in the mirror and saw a dead sister?

7

Lullwater Review, Crab Orchard Review, Pegasus,
Maverick Duck Press, Main Street Rag, The Moccasin,
Lachryma, Katydid, Nimrod, Taproot, Seaweed Sideshow Circus,
Bottom Dog Press, Milkweed Editions,
Red Moon—I could make a poem
out of the places that have returned my poems.
How can they travel to Raintown
or Chattahoochee or Cimarron or Cream City
or Cold Mountain or the River Styx or the Pleiades
and not be changed?
Adastra, Anabiosis, Anhinga, Apalachee, Aquarius, Axe Factory.
I'm working my way through the alphabet.
Every time I go to the mailbox
I'm one step closer to *Zephyr Quarterly, Zilch Magazine,*
Zombie Logic Press, and a world record.
How many people can brag they've been rejected
by *The Unmuzzled Ox, Tickled by Thunder,*
The Eclectic Muse, Goose Lane Editions,
Hippopotamus Press, Frogmore, Lapwing?

8

If a man writes 2 poems a week for 50 years—
take away 1 poem for every week
his hands got distracted
with the papier-mâché Mt.Vesuvius his daughter was molding
or a fort he was building with his Cub Scouts
or a protest sign he held up before the State House—
and you do the math:
52 weeks times 2 poems a week equals 104
minus 15 neglected poems equals 89
times 50 years equals 4,450
minus 52 for the long year his mother took to die
minus 26 for the long year his father took to die.

That leaves 4,372 poems by the time he's 70.
Maybe 400 or so, if he's lucky, make their way
into print, which leaves 3,972 poems
just waiting to be thrown away when he dies.
But, look, he's at work on yet another poem.

9

Why do I keep writing?
Maybe because words ask the same toughness
of an old man or woman as they would of a young one:
to be seventy—or eighty or ninety—
and still be held to a code
of honor. Poems don't want excuses.

10

The trees must have noticed
my attention wandering.
I look out the window to find them
holding up their latest work.
Their first drafts have turned incandescent.
Who'd believe anything as ordinary
as a maple could have such an extraordinary vocabulary,
redolent with so many variations of red and orange
and yellow. While I've been dawdling,
the trees have been busy revising.
The light's the only critic they trust.
They count on the sun
to polish their scribbling, to see their first drafts
all the way to print. What would we ever do
without such independent publishers?

From
THE FIRST INHABITANTS OF ARCADIA

(University of Arkansas Press, 2006)

The Visitor

On the morning before Dr. Johnson died
a stranger, a near-blind girl, pushed into his bedroom.
Even before his friends suspected
that she had opened the front door, she had
lifted the small, troubled congregation of his huge fingers
and held them to her face and demanded
the great man bless her. Only a week before,
the author of *The Vanity of Human Wishes*
had urged the physician's hand
to stab deeper, lancing the swollen leg.
To go to the root of the infection?
To cut away all that was vile in him?
Later, he had found scissors and drove them into his calf.
What did he mean by damnation?
Sent to Hell, Sir, and punished everlastingly.
Now barely able to shape his breath
into sounds, he—
already convinced
of his own irredeemable wickedness—
did bless her as if he had decided to believe
that words still had a right
to do that: not heal, but make tolerable;
not lighten the load, but enable one to
take up its heavy weight; not restore sight,
but help one bear not seeing.

What If You Could Be Any Letter?

The world was all before them, where to choose
Their place of rest and providence their guide:
They hand in hand with wandering steps and slow
Through Eden took their solitary way.
                    —Paradise Lost, Book XII

Once again my students in jail look at me as if I'm crazy,
but they do what I ask. It just so happens,
they remind me, that they aren't going anywhere
for the next 4-6 years. I've worn down their ringleader
till finally he's willing to be a little silly. From here on
even the Warden will have to address Jason as *S*
as, he says, in *stealth, sly, slick.* Once I've got him on my side
the rest join in. *S*'s buddy, Trey,
is *T*, the bodybuilder, the muscleman.
Eric, the one the rest call Mouse,
lingers over the letter *R*
because his grandmother used to call him Little Ricky
till he'd been arrested so many times she gave up on him.

Eugene decides to be silent *e*, not a bad choice
for a pickpocket. Pete and Roberto got busted twice
together. They're always quarreling,
inseparable even in jail, so we tease and call them the dynamic duo,
Q and *U*. The smash-and-grabber, Daniel, is *D*
because he doesn't have much imagination,
a fact which explains why he keeps getting caught.
We get into an argument over *C*. It's *K*
in disguise, says Eliot, the stockbroker
serving 3-5 for supplementing his income
with cocaine. *It's cagey. It's crafty.*
A cut-throat. A conniver. Coldblooded.
It's chaos. It's catastrophe.

Most of the men gathered at the table
are here because they heard the ladies might be allowed
to come to this class, but now
that they're stuck with me, we get down to work.
At least here they get college credit for engaging in fantasy.
Today I want them to pretend the planet is doomed
and there's just one spaceship
and they've got to choose who lives and who doesn't.
(It beats mopping floors or dishing out potatoes.)

The world was always coming to an end
when I was a kid, and there was no time to talk
about anything else. *A meteor is heading for the earth,*
I'd say to the boy that my mother had made me play with
because she was friends with his mother.
We've got the last rocket. There's not enough
for your whole family. Pick someone.
We spent the afternoon deciding
whom and what we'd save, which books to take.
That was one of the rules.
We had to lug language on board.

Imagine that we're drifting in space.
What do we do to pass the time?
I now ask Tiny, the 300 lb. check forger,
and Moon, the second-story man,
and Steve M, the shoplifter and Steve R. the carjacker,
and Phil who fell asleep in the house he was robbing.
Tomorrow I'll get one man remembering
the aunt who taught him to cook;
another, the long year his father wouldn't speak to him.
I sit with a third and together we try to
recall snow falling on water,
or what rain really tastes like.
For a few minutes we decide to pretend
this is the real purpose of life:

floating away not just from the prison
but the planet and looking back at the earth
from our space station, giving up
on the mother ship ever remembering to return for us.
We've got no supplies,
just this intrepid crew. *A, B, C, D, E, F, G, H, I, J, K,*
L, M, N, O, P, Q, R, S, T, U, V, W,
X, Y, Z, the first inhabitants of Arcadia,
now homesick, curious exiles from Eden,
navigating their valiant path through the universe,
always looking back
over their shoulders at Paradise.

Multiple Personality Disorder

Time? In junior high I had so much
         on my hands
    I invented
theories about the letters
         in the alphabet
    and the lives they led,
especially the ingenuity required
         of a vowel, silent
    e, for example. It had no
choice but to adapt to every
         sort of circumstance:
    one moment the demure
domestic, able to endure any
         indignity; the next
    a hunched-over magician with
power to transform *trip*
         into *tripe, slop*
    into *slope, fat* into
fate, crap into *crape.* One more
         of *e*'s sleight-
    of-hand tricks: Now it's a *shame;*
now it's a *sham.* Tricky
         e disguised as *y*?
    Determined *e* im-
personating *u*? Lowercase *e*
         with its MPD, just part
    of a large family used to wearing
each other's clothes, bumping
         into themselves,
    molecules
crammed into a too-small room,
         language
    not knowing what
else to do but talk
         to itself. Long
    to short. Short to
silent.

F

F, one more letter that deserves a whole book devoted to it,
                the alphabet's Little Lord
Fauntleroy, flaunting its frills, its French cuffs, its fluency
                in many languages, flamboyant
fricative I fell for the way other boys fall for football players,
                infatuated with the
figure it cut, uppercase *F* I'd write over and over
                just to feel it
float over the page as some suitors might fill whole notebooks
                with their beloved's
full name—though I was even more fond of small-case
                f, its ferocity, its
fealty, the way it faced facts, let its faith be tested,
                how it refused to
flinch, the teeth biting the lower lip, the air
                forced out, the sigh that
finishes so many words, first part of so many oaths
                for God and country,
for chrissake, for pity's sake, forswearing all others,
                forsaking no one,
forever true, the perfect letter for a fourteen-year-old—though
                how's he going to admit
falling so in love with a consonant, he'd fain die
                for it, that old
fop of a letter, fatalist, finagler, freedom fighter, fancy pants,
                the way it
flounces, flicks its hips, stretches out its arms, flings itself
                forward into the future.

Ode to *J*

just as often bouncing a little ball
                off its nose
        as about to e-
ject from its seat, it teaches the frogs to
                jet-propel off
        their lily pads, the pond to
jitterbug, the rain to
                appreciate its own
        jive, the storm to stop apolo-
gizing. By junior high I'd tired
                of words, their bullying
        justifications, glittering
generalities. I'd forgotten
                about the revelry
        certain letters enga-
ge in, their jujitsu, jam sessions, juicy
                stories, the secret
        delights of jealousy
and bad jokes. How could I give up hope
                in a world where
        j's the silent letter in mari-
juana? It jostles. It jars.
                What's a kid to do
        but take all the
joy he can, light up a joint,
                jack off,
        jiggle the brain,
jolt the body? Juggler, jester
                renegade *i*,
        the alphabet's adopted child,
j's got the tongue talking
                to the roof of the mouth,
        a new kind of
justice, something as common
                as air
        turned into
jubilation. The brain
                has precious few
        pleasures and *j*,
jocund, jaunty
                j, is one of them.

Letter *L* as in Reliable, Indomitable, Chivalrous

It's hard not to like
     L. Life.
   Love. Luck. It's so full
of lofty ideals. A natural born leader
     of all the laggard
   vowels: lugubrious *u,*
ever-loitering *e,* loopy *o*
   it makes sure
isn't left behind. Think,
     L seems to say,
   of all you can accomplish
if you work as diligently
     as an adverb.
   It latches on
to an adjective and sweetly,
     softly, almost indiscernibly,
   persuades it to
spread its goodwill to the rest
     of the sentence.
   Lambent. Luminous.
Lucent. What pleasure there is
     in working certain words
   into sentences. *L* changes
everything. Unflinching-
     ly, unstintingly, it labors:
   Let the earth
put forth vegetation, plants
     yielding seed, and fruit trees
   fruit in which is their seed.
That's not just the Lord
     talking. That's
   language. *Let there be...*
How lovely it feels
     to tuck the tongue
   against the teeth
and let the lungs do the rest.

Babbadino

Babbadino, me babbadino,
Zack says, his mouth pressed to my ear
as if he's not going to trust the air
to carry the words he's just learned:
Babbadino me. You can't go to a store with Zack
and not come back without something that bounces
and has stars on it. An earth with air inside it.
A wiffle ball. A nerf ball. A super ball
that can be squeezed inside a two-year old's palm
and yet can hurdle whole buildings.
God knew what he was doing when He invented
rubber. What more could one ask for
than something squishy that jumps out of your hands
and hops down the sidewalk
as if it has someplace important to go
and it's your job to follow it. *Zack—*
a fist of consonants, capital *Z* marching out to meet all
who dare approach. *Zack—*
a kid who'll forge his own destiny:
a catcher who'll work his way up from the minors;
a tough negotiator who'll settle age-old conflicts
between warring states; a congressman
known for his principles. Right now Zack's too busy
to worry about the future
his father's picked out for him. He's marveling
at the miracle of roundness
we call a ball and he calls a *babbadino.*
Some kids are like that: you've got to scoop them up,
bounce them on your knee,
then put them back on the floor. You treat them
with the same respect and affection
you would a ball. Zack's blissfully intent
on the ball rolling in and out of his hands.
Babbadino! Zack will shout into my ear
as if *ball* is not a round enough word
for something that caroms
off walls, windows, ceilings, something so marvelous
it could roll and roll
forever, if it wished, and maybe today
it will. It's not going to let anything get in its way.

At Any Early Age a Boy Discovers the Pleasures
and Perils of Double *O*

Put these silly identical twins
        o and *o*
    in a word and it goes goofy,
but endearing. *Buffoon.*
        Booby. Nincompoop.
      Your mother's not crazy,
just a little loony. That's not shit
        in your pants
    but poopy.
Add one more *o* to lose
        and you're loose
    and ashamed
of nothing but ready
        for everything: *Cookie!*
    Snookie! Whoopie! Booze!
Floozies! Words only too willing
        to pooh-pooh
    the alphabet's great aspirations,
that silly goose. How far
        would you get with a girl
    if seduce were spelled
sedoos? What conclusions
        would a philosopher
    dedoos? What if
there were nothing loopy
        in the language, no
    va-va voom? No magic
broom. No swooping wings?
        No dark lagoon?
    No fingernail
moon? No freedom to *ooh*
        and *ahh,* to swoon.
    Nothing too
gorgeous for words?
        Too, small extremist,
    pipsqueak adverb, always
piping up: *Too much?*
        There's never
    too much!

The Pathetic Fallacy

His bedroom was filled with gallon jugs
of urine he wouldn't let any of his visitors throw away,
a sort of maze we, his students, had to pass through
to get to him. Was he still testing us, bottle
by bottle, a gallant troop, a private army, his palace guards?
Nearly blind with most of his heart
man-made, two cancers under his belt,
he had suffered so much that we'd forgotten
how each illness required new courage
of this sweet grammarian who had tutored us with such devotion
that we had often confused him
with the language he'd tried to improve
in us. There are plenty of elegies for young
drowned men, but how many for the prematurely
old surrounding themselves with bottles of urine
as though they now expected
a conflagration so terrible they'd have to
rely on their own body's fluids
to put it out, gallon after gallon, their last defense?

***

The Saint Meets His Match, The Saint Goes Underground,
Pope's translation of *The Aeneid,*
The Collected Trollope, the last five issues of *Baseball Digest,*
a whole library of French semanticists
piled on the hospital bed,
on the rolling table. If he was going to be attached
to machines, tubes running into all kinds of places
on him, he refused to suffer
alone. He brought Sir Philip Sydney for company,
Samuel Daniel, Edmund Waller.
Coleridge shared his bed along with Flannery O'Connor
and John Woolman. If he ever was going to indulge himself,
what better time? On the bureau:
The Lysistrata, The Inferno (in three translations), *Paradise Lost*
and *The Life and Death of Buddy Holly,*
books heaped so high
it looked as if he was conducting an experiment
to test precisely how long
before everything collapses.

***

Dead?
       Dead!
Why any of you could be dead,
pipes a bird cheerily
as if no other morning existed but this,
no other branch but this very one.
Listen, that bird knows Elizabethan poetry better
than most of us. No, I'm serious.
Who else hooked up to an IV,
surrounded by young men who adored him,
would be arguing the merits of the Pathetic Fallacy?
You flatter me too much,
blushes the rose. *O how you do go on!*
insist those little hypocrites, the daffodils.

***

At nineteen to be allowed to call my professor
Bob! To fold his wheelchair
into the back of my car, see that he got where he needed,
and pretend that only I could get him there!
Once he clutched for his chest
and I thought he was having another heart attack,
but he was only grasping for one of those notebooks
he'd go nowhere without,
like a lung he carried in his breast pocket,
another way of breathing, translating
Molière, Goethe, Thucydides, Gershwin,
Conway Twitty, Sister Sledge, Richie Ashburn, Dr J.,
Latin derivations, malapropisms from student essays,
Fulke Greville, the Marx brothers,
a miniature blueprint for a medieval castle,
malapropisms from student essays,
a few calculus problems still to work out,
all in a brown spiral notebook. He even had one in his robe
at hospice. Dying was not going to stop him
from writing down everything
he was determined not to forget.

***

Don't argue with me. I did see Jesus,
Fraser said with such conviction it was hard to remember
that here was the same person who had trouble
buying a pair of shoes. He absolutely believed

in the music of the spheres, the genius
of doo-wop, and the transfiguration of Christ,
and he tried to persuade each of us
as if offering a gift he was so excited about
he'd started unwrapping it himself. *This is it,* he'd say
to a kid with blue hair sitting on his bed,
and he'd turn up the small tape recorder he'd taken everywhere.
Follow the tenor. Notice how he starts as backup
and then takes over the song,
how the lead singer defers to him.
He's got the voice of someone who's drowned
and been brought back to life. You're right,
it is another language at first.
Okay, this is the only decent song
on the album. But it is really good.
It is extraordinary. There is nothing quite like it.

***

How is the professor doing? we'd ask.
Now that he was dying, we'd stopped calling him
Bob, except when we were helping him
to the john. It hurt him even to piss.
He had to think hard
to move muscles he shouldn't have had to worry about.
And so he dragged his wounded body closer
and closer to the ledge, and then one morning
shut his eyes and let himself fall.

***

The cords of death encompassed me.
The torrents of perdition assailed me.
The cords of Sheol entangled me.
The snares of death confronted me.
In my distress I called upon the Lord.

***

The trees clustered like a family of mourners
who'd not be consoled. After the service
we walked in the sunlit garden,
wiping our foreheads, complaining of the heat
because we had to talk about something. Each of us had to
look somewhere, so I chose to stare

at the flowers, the way the wind made quiet inquiries of the grass
and the way the grass answered
demurely, the branches trembling
faintly as if someone who'd passed there
had brushed them aside. Was it a ghost?
No, only another breeze
eavesdropping, a merry
impish, lilac-petaled breeze lingering
to hear what a man will think up to praise it.

Say the Magic Word

Cottage cheese? Special noodles?
   No, thank you.
Juice in your favorite cup?
   No, thank you.
Toast cut into soldiers?
   No, thank you.
To be not quite two and free
   to say *no* all day
and add *thank you,*
   so endearingly reasonable
that no can argue with you,
   as if all that's required
is to be gracious and wait
   for the world
to do its part. Even on this rainy day
   when you wake up
before you're ready to
   and nothing sounds good
and you're tired of this large person
   who talks too loud
like a used-car salesman:
   Pears and Chicken?
No, thank you! Sweet potatoes
   and ham? *No,*
thank you! Till you must wonder
   if he's slow-witted
and if this world's not all
   that it seemed
just a few minutes ago.
   And then there it is,
exactly what you wanted: Macaroni
   and Cheese,
and the man you call OPA,
   because you like the *O*
floating in the air till the *P*
   gets impatient
to be spoken and the *A*'s a question
   waiting for its answer
—blows on the macaroni
   and you blow too, because it's fun

to do what Opa does. It's so easy
         to get him laughing,
that must be one of your purposes
         in this life. And his is
to drop everything and run
         when you say his name.
What a life this is! More milk
         than you can drink,
five kinds of cereal, a whole box
         of colors all yours
to do with as you wish, a blanket
         that smells of sleep,
dollies that let you undress them,
         and everyone ready to tell you
what a good job you did
         in your diapers,
rub cream on you and let you
         sprinkle powder
on the cat. And apparently
         this will go on
forever and ever, it seems,
         world
without end.

What's Missing in the Dictionary

What did Webster know of the sound
        of sand packed around you,
of being nothing but a head
        on a beach? The way your feet revel
in mud, the delicious pleasure
        of getting stuck and unstuck.
Even the O.E.D. has no term
        for snow under your collar
or the sting of soda bubbles
        up your nose. Not even a phrase
for what rain smells like
        before it falls
or what got you through the day
        your grandfather died.
What's the Latin for the stretching
        of time after a boy's best friend
leaves for camp, or the compressing
        of a whole childhood
into one dive into trees
        reflected in a pond,
those rapturous seconds
        when a girl breaks surface
and knows that she can do this again
        and again? There ought to be
a better word for what a kid does
        alone with his own body.
How about *Ooolalala*
        or *About time?*
What does Webster have to say
        about wiping clean your father's
buttocks, or holding your son as he flails
        in the water? Or watching your lover
lose his hair, or a friend get the award
        you'd hoped to win,
or a bird peck at the hard ground
        as if it owes him something
and he isn't going to stop till
        he's got what's his?

From
THE IMPROBABLE SWERVINGS OF ATOMS

(University of Pittsburgh Press, 2005)

The Soul Wants the Last Word

If you can't trust me, whom can you
        trust? says
   the soul, that bully
with his Bhavagad Gita,
        that Jungian therapist,
   transcendental
thug, maharishi
       in circus tights,
   who's tricked you up so high
you can't get down.
        Let yourself go,
   says the *Here.*
What are you waiting for?
        asks the *Now.*
   Meaning: jump in the water
though it's miles over your head.
        Meaning: open the door
   of the airplane
and see if the air respects your self-
       actualization.
   You've got to live
in the moment,
        says the soul.
   It's got wings
and is ready
        to take you
   for a ride.
So what if you can't breathe?
        So what
   if there's too much light
to see. It's put on sunglasses.
        It's turned up the music.
   Don't look down,
it says. *Whatever you do*
        don't
   look down.

Why I Hate Math

The day my daughter was hit by a car,
approximately 38,550 children died of hunger and hunger-
related diseases. It didn't matter how many times
that her mother and I had warned Nora
about the street. Being four and so enchanted
by her game, she forgot
that anything could hurt her,
especially the car that did. I wouldn't speak of this
if she'd been killed. I am not one of the unlucky
parents who did all they could to keep their children
safe, only to lose a son
or daughter anyway. To what?
Cancer? Spinal Meningitis? Famine? War? Accident?
The laws of percentages?
Some nights the house gets so dark
I have to claw my way out of
a dream and bump against sofa, piano, bookcase
to my daughter's room. I used to be secretly glad
my wife couldn't breast-feed.
I loved the kiss of the first few drops from the bottle
on my wrist, the little reassuring
scalding that reminded me that even though I was half-asleep,
I was doing my best to make sure that it was me
who got burned, not my child.
At 3 a.m. I'd hold the baby
so tight, it was almost as if she was drinking
from my body. All my shirts smelled
of milk and spit-up. In the middle of a difficult meeting
or stuck in traffic, all I had to do was breathe
deeply, and Nora would be so real
I'd look down, surprised
she wasn't in my arms. I labored under the assumption
that if I tried my hardest, life would
reward me, keep the pavement from bruising my child,
the fire from leaping off the stove,
lightning from striking. I learned
what all parents must: All the worry, all the vigilance
in a moment cancelled out, and there's nothing
one can do. One might as well try to argue with an equation.
No court of appeal, no retribution.
Just ruthless algebra.

August 6

Lie down on the street! I tell my son,
so he takes off his jacket
and methodically, the way he's learned at Cub Scouts,
folds it smaller and smaller, like a flag,
and then it turns into a pillow.
My daughter, usually wanting nothing more
than to do what her brother just did,
follows his example and folds her hands so tightly over her chest,
the left and the right seem afraid
to let go of each other. We look up at the clouds
and wait for them to tell us something
they haven't yet. The street is full of bodies
pretending to be stricken, trying to
be as dead as they can, though soon my son grows bored
with his own dying and is ready to
get back to what no one can beat him at:
systematically, ingeniously
tormenting his sister and then teasing her even more
for crying. Then a siren tears open the heavens.
The doves, set loose, swirl above us, dive and rise
as if the earth's on fire and there's nowhere
safe to alight. My son stretches his hand up
into the air. My daughter does the same.
If her brother's just done it, then it must be important to do.
It's obvious that they can't grasp anything
but air, though when did that ever stop a kid
from reaching his arm up
to pluck a hawk from the clouds,
seize a shooting star? That old lie of perspective, deceit
of vision, one more betrayal
kids never get used to. On the stage
a man with no legs is embracing a man
with no eyes, but we are gazing past them to the darkening sky.
Today we hold it responsible
not only for the storm about to scatter us,
the cops fidgety as winds and just as trigger happy,
but for everything gone wrong in the universe.

Utopia

In the next fifty minutes create a perfect world.
Be sure to proofread.

So what if their utopias occasionally drop the ending
for the past tense or dangle participles?
At least they will have managed, all by themselves
in the next hour,
            to cure cancer and AIDS.
And if the sentences in which they distribute wealth equally,
clean up the rivers, wipe out racism,
and put an end to crime as well as invent a drug
that's not addictive or expensive, but just as eye-opening
as LSD, and, while they're at it, outlaw
political parties and final exams
            run on,
what's the big deal? Your students aren't interested
in anything as petty as punctuation.
In the kingdom created by the girl
whose grandmother has been dying all semester,
no one uses semicolons and everyone gets to
turn into whatever they wish. *It's not like reincarnation,*
she writes. *You get to remember your past existence*
and you go back to being who you were
if you're tired of being a lizard or a lake.
            No one hurts anyone
in the anorexic's utopia, but if they do
they get nails driven into their palms
and are hung in the city square.
            Ask for imagination
and expect consistency? The President of the Young Republicans'
top priority is equality. In his planetary nudist colony,
everyone's forbidden from wearing a stitch of clothes.
The marketing major's a hermit. The art major wants money
harvested like marijuana, field after field
of hundred dollar bills. He grows fabulously wealthy
right before your eyes.
            No matter how often
you write *See me!* on the essays
of the young man who always is talking about Jesus,
you can't get him to stick to a thesis.
There is no such thing as expository writing
in his heaven. *It's* valleys are verdant green.

He's not worried about redundancy
or apostrophes in Paradise.
        Utopia
for the kid just out of reform school
is the backwoods behind a quarry
where he's free to ride dirt bikes and dive off cliffs.
The water's torn and heals itself
all day. Maybe it's not the end of the world
if he can't get *their* and *there* straight.
        After the class,
the kid who always wears his Yankees hat backwards
lifts his shirt to show you exactly where,
on his stomach,
        the medicine gets pumped in.
His utopia brims with light
the color of insulin. His roads have no traffic.

Singing Yourself Down the Stairs

How long can this young man hold his club over my head
before his arm grows so tired, he's got to
bring it down, let it do
                    what it was meant to do,
teach the back of my neck a lesson it won't
soon forget?
                    No blood for oil!
What was I thinking when I made the sign?
That the cops would read
what I'd written and go and tell the President?
                    No more napalm!
No more body bags! Was I foolish enough to believe
that people at home getting supper, singing
to their babies, running the bathwater,
would glance up at their television sets
and see words held high on sticks
and say, *Oh yes, we have to change our lives!*
Maybe the cop who's looking straight at me
as if he'd kill me if he could
                    get away with it
did the same thing as I did last night: sang
his son in and out of his bath
and then sang himself down the stairs,
no different from any father
who, having argued with the monsters in his child's room,
wants the last word and
                    that word to be song,
not because singing makes the dark
any less dark, the cold less determined to
infiltrate our bones, not because song wins
any concessions from a congress
of cancer cells or has any hope of bringing
peace on earth, but because words, by themselves, are
not enough. The only god I could tolerate
would be one who sings
                    to himself,
part guffaw, part trembling, part whistle,
part wail because it's the only way he can
bear all the empty places he can't fill, the unrelenting,
                    infinitely
irreconcilable universe. And so the father sings.
                    And so the son.

College Professor Suspended

Semulkahn, three years away from her native Liberia,
bends over her blue book
with the concentration of someone trying to land a plane
in a pasture. Stochko, the paraplegic,
wears Hawaiian shirts so outrageous
he's obviously making a point:
So what if I'm in a wheelchair?
I still can be gorgeous as a tropical bird.
Ankit presses so close to his exam book, it's a door
he's trying to push open.
Winston lifts his head, takes a gulp of air
and then dives back into his essay.
So what if he can't speak a simple sentence
without stuttering? Rachel,
the kid who spent the last ten years in foster care,
jumps on her midterm
as someone might a horse she intends to ride hard
into the sunset. Every few minutes
she digs her spurs in. Peter's tossing his hair back.
It keeps getting between him
and what he wants to say. It's so dark and wavy
all the girls want to run their fingers
through it. Even the teacher has all he can do
to keep his hands out of its tangles.
Why should it shock anyone that a teacher might wish to
lie down with one of his students?
The girl whispering to the words she writes
as if to coax them out of hiding.
The boy who's said nothing all term
but whose thoughts rush onto the paper now
like water out of a faucet, spilling over, reveling in the fact
of all this empty space, the unexpected freedom
of the page. The heroin addict.
The baseball pitcher, who one day confesses to the class
his dad's a drunk. *That's why I never tell him*
the day I'm gonna start.
The girl who's got gum stuck in her hair.
The pimply kid who strokes his ankle as he writes,
the one smooth part
left to his body. *All that nakedness*
mine, thinks the teacher.

E Pluribus Unum

Just what's going on in that thick skull
of yours? asks the teacher, and it takes you a while to figure out
that he's talking to you, and though you're tempted
to tell him that you are, in fact, contemplating
United States history, you don't
because football practice is next
and what is going through your head
is a locker room full of naked presidents,
all the Jameses and Johns showering together.
When you'd got on the school bus this morning,
you didn't plan to think about Grover Cleveland
scrubbing Chester Arthur's back,
or Millard Fillmore letting his towel fall away
so there's no mistaking his most democratic part,
or Monroe scratching his balls
as if that was his manifest destiny. How is a boy to explain
that he's got Quincy Adams' testicles
on his mind and Warren Harding's buttocks?
When Thomas Jefferson bends over
you can almost see into the darkness
that fills the third President of the United States.
What did you expect? That George Washington
would be all padding like your grandmother?
Did you doubt that a man in a wig
would have the same parts as you, more
or less? Poor penis,
who wouldn't wish to comfort such a wobbly thing
no matter what wars it waged or whom it managed
to exterminate. Teddy Roosevelt's can't help
saluting to the Republic. Eisenhower's just lolls there
as if it's earned the right to do nothing
presidential for a while. What hope is there for you
if this is the kind of thing you're going to imagine?
Rutherford B. Hayes letting the water
have its way with him?
Woodrow Wilson drawing faces in the mirror's steam
as if even the Leader of the Free World gets tired
of being serious all the time? Today in Room 203,

all of American history comes down to
a boy thinking things
he shouldn't and knowing not to say anything, no matter
how hard he's pressed.

De Rerum Natura

...the funeral song is mingled
With the cry of babies come to the shores of light.

It's the perfect book if you're thinking of killing yourself
but don't really want to, if you'd like to
believe in God but find Him
even more daunting than that erector set
you got one Christmas, all those complicated instructions
when really all you wanted to do was
screw one shiny metal thing to another. If despair's
your only true principle, if you're convinced
that the world's an awful place,
Lucretius won't try to sway you
from your allegiances. He provides more than enough
pestilence, war, disease
to satisfy the most confirmed pessimist:
The throat oozes black blood, the tongue drips gore,
The dogs stretch flat on the street and lay down their sick souls,
And the bodies of lifeless parents are heaped
On the lifeless bodies of children.
Yet right after *the temples become charnel houses,*
there Lucretius is, on the next page,
giving a lecture on meteorology, saying *Gee whiz*
in Latin, like the biggest dork on the earth,
a professor so excited about his lab experiment
he stops worrying whether the students are awake
or not. He can't get over the vacuum
that makes life so interesting:
how the atoms have to keep filling it
in new and unpredictable ways. If you want a reason
to go on living, even in the midst
of a long and protracted war, it's the magnet,
Stone at which you gape in wonder....
You can link rings in a chain suspended from it,
And sometimes you'll see five or even more
Dangle in order and sway in the light breeze,
One ring depending on the next, as each
Communicates with the magnet's binding force
And clings—such potency seeps through them all.
Once you get Lucretius started,
there's no stopping him. He's like a kid fallen

so in love that nothing makes sense now
except in reference to the one he's besotted with. *Magnets!*
Remember those little dogs
that kids used to play with, pulling the white terrier
from the black, then making it fly smack into the other
as if there were no end to the pleasure
of investigation: hypotheses you had to keep testing over and over,
the air first charged with the power
of refusal, then the irresistible embrace, north seeking south.
south seeking north, crazed lovers,
the urgent kiss of metal
against metal? Were these little Scotties
really teaching boys and girls the facts of life?
Maybe kids wouldn't get so screwed up
if they kept up their religious studies
of magnetism. After all, Lucretius died only a few years
before Christ was born. Maybe the cross
is a kind of magnet. Drugs are, surely. And porn.
Maybe it's not just okay to be pulled
toward the very thing that you know
you must resist. Maybe
it's a law of physics. Open *De Rerum Natura*
to Book Six, if you are not sure
that life's worth living, if you're torn this way and that.
Look, Lucretius says, it's all possible
because there's so much space
to be filled and it gets really crowded
with all those plagues and priests
telling everyone what to believe. *But—*
how the author of The Nature of Things loves this word—
consider how porous it all is,
how there's always room
for atoms to do what they have their hearts set
on doing: finding windows
to slip in and out of, *secret passages,*
whole highways, pipes up our Roman troublemaker,
in things that look so solid
nothing could get through, doors flung open
where no doors seem possible.

42 Linden

Live! Learn! Worship! Shop!
—The Paradise Chamber of Commerce

1

The Promised Land Mall. The Elysian Fields Spa.
The Shangri-la Delicatessen.
Of course it got out of hand. Who wouldn't want to
make a buck or two off the other world?
Take a right at Celestial, go straight past Olympus,
Valhalla, and Nirvana,
and you can't miss Harry's Heavenly Hotdogs,
Galilee Plastics, River Jordan Wingnuts,
Mt. Sinai Waste Management Corp.
Who wouldn't find the ironies delicious
if Paradise had more than its share
of embezzlers, check forgers, inside traders, wives
who sleep with their gardeners.
However, mostly it's just a working-class community.
Children, tired of their homework, listen to acid rock
while they load and unload their father's collection of antique guns,
and everyone goes on being born
and dying at the appointed times on Apostle Drive
or the Blessed Martyrs Boulevard.

2

As soon as their wives and kids drive off to church,
the men on streets named after trees and flowers and fruits
head for the cellar and their train sets, the hills
they've molded so softly rolling to a sea
that not even God could have done a better job.
On the seventh day none of them rest; instead
they search the house for the right screwdriver,
the precise wrench size. Every week
comes down to this: oiling the tiny gears
that keep the world and its railroads running.
The milk car must deliver its miniature silver cans at 48 Fleur-de-Lis.
The cattle car has a quota it must honor on 76 Hyacinth.
Tiny sacks of mail. Tiny logs. Tinier coal.
Beneath 42 Linden's house, too, there's track
to be laid, mountains to be raised,
tunnels to be dug through them.
Fields expect their fair share of flowers;
rivers demand to be carved out of the land.

The sun must be set in the heavens,
and the moon can't wait. It's got to see to make sure
that the tides come in and go out on schedule.

3

Imagine buying up so much land
you're free to name every body of water, every hill
on it, turn what was a Sodom and Gomorrah
of sumac and poison ivy
into a heaven on which anyone could put down a deposit,
uproot the degeneracy of vines, their illicit embraces.
Whoever laid out the traffic patterns in Paradise
didn't want to leave anything to chance:
so in the Nightingale section every street begins with *N*;
with an *O* in Oriole Glen; in Periwinkle no road's permitted
to start with anything but P and from there
you turn into Quail Hollow,
then Rambling Rose, then Snowball Gate,
and then Tamarisk. What fun
to be in charge of the language, to have the alphabet
all one's own to do with as one wishes.

4

It's not April, yet at 44 Linden Drive a boy's
already half-naked, on the theory,
perhaps, that if he acts like it's spring,
then spring will get the picture
and come when the boy wants it, which is now,
shooting hoops in his driveway
in a town someone had the hubris to name
Paradise. He could be any one of a number of boys
tired of gravity, free-throws against his father's garage,
but right now he's the savior
in gym shorts, leading his people out of Egypt
as the ball finds its way back
to the promised land. What's sweeter
than hitting nothing but strings?
The bonus to a jump shot: watching it
jostle the net, the space still filled
by what's just fallen through it, that lovely illusion
of closure, and the boy wants it
again and again, and he'll shoot lay-ups, finger-rolls, skyhooks
till he gets it back, no pleasure ever enough,
even in Paradise.

5

When he lived in the city, Apt. 3B grew so used to worrying
that it stopped being worried. It's what he did:
he woke the kids up, got their breakfast,
saw to it that they brushed their teeth,
and pulled them out of the way of oncoming cars.
But now he's 42 Linden Boulevard,
and here the streets have such pretty names:
Lily of the Valley Lane, Honey Locust Hollow.
It's a wonder cars dare drive down them.
Maybe he moved here because he believed
in the power of language. If his kids played on streets
named Frankincense, Sandalwood, Quince
and all in a town called Paradise,
how could any irreparable harm befall them?
What does it matter if quince doesn't thrive
in these parts, if there is no persimmon
on Persimmon Court? Mahogany Road, Rosewood Drive
Teak Court, no day complete without the elegant furnishings
of trees, their dark, alluvial grains.

6

Night after night 42 Linden stands just outside
his children's room and, because he can't hear anything,
listens even harder, convinced that it's out there—
whatever wants to hurt his kids—
and he's got to be ready to throw himself in front of it,
whatever it is. What if he were to screw up
and lose his job and have to explain to his children
why they must say goodbye to gardens
and golf courses? So 42 Linden never rests.
The way a blade of grass, every second of every minute,
reminds itself not to loosen its grip
on its little piece of property. The way a babbling brook works
its full-time job rushing the same direction
day in and day out. You can't be too careful.
Even in Paradise. Especially in Paradise.

7

Sometimes the worry gets too much for 42 Linden
and so he makes up excuses
to get up from the floor where he's been crayoning
with his kids. There's something broken he's been meaning to fix.

The boy next door is jumping into the sky,
and it takes 42 Linden a moment
to realize that the kid's just snagging a rebound.
The kid's shoulders glisten. Today he's not skin and bones
that happened to get bad grades in Algebra
and have acne. Today the sun turns every blotch on the boy's face
irrelevant. Day and night he's out there
throwing a ball against the rim,
sometimes even trying to miss, teaching his hands
what to do when he's way off the mark.
The boy never seems to get tired of chasing down his mistakes.
He seems born to do this: scoop up a ball in his hands
and lift off the earth as if he knows
that this is the closest he's ever going to come to having wings.

8

On Monday 42 Linden Drive packs lunches for his kids.
On Tuesday he leads his Cub Scouts in the Pledge of Allegiance.
On Wednesday he marks his students'
essays: B+, B/B-, C+, A++ —that crazy enterprise
of pretending one can put a grade on anything.
Thursday he takes a neighbor to the hospital
though her husband's out on the lawn shouting
he's learned his lesson, he won't do it again.
On Friday 42 Linden gets home early so he can leave his wife
at her job at the lab and pick up the kids
and still have time with them, at dusk,
to throw stones into the river
till everything grows dark and finally they can see
distances only by hearing them, the splash each rock makes.

9

Put in Paradise, how many of us wouldn't return
to our old occupations: if you were a burglar
testing the locks, trying the windows;
if you were a retired plumber, making work
out of the smallest of jobs;
if you're a father doing what you do best—worrying;
if you were a child of an alcoholic, second-guessing everything,
undermining your best intentions?
That night 42 Linden's wife moves her hands over him
with the quiet authority of water,
the way water's able to find every hollow

and crevice and fill it, and yet no matter how grateful
42 Linden is, his mind wanders.
Now it's the furious self-importance
of a stone skimmed over a creek.
Now, it's the sound of pages being flipped,
his four-year-old daughter's ritual
after she's been kissed goodnight and the door's closed,
reading book after book
till she falls asleep in mid-sentence.
Now it's the way the ball keeps persuading the strings
to let it drop through the exact center,
the way a kid's already under the net waiting
for his last shot to fall back into his hands
as it's never enough to do something perfectly
just once, you've got to do it again
and again. Even as 42 Linden's wife seems to pour herself
over him, even as he opens his legs
to take her in, he can hear the ball bouncing
off the rim. Is it all right
in Paradise to go on dreaming of still another paradise?
That's what 42 Linden would like to know.
He's a child being rescued from a sinking ship.
He's a boy carried off by a bird
and set down in the lap of the clouds.
He's a young man plummeting through a sky
so immense he could fall forever.

From
OVID AT FIFTEEN

(New Issues Western Michigan University, 2003)

Ovid At Fifteen

1

Not another naked woman
    sprouting roots,
  the kid in front of you moans,
your classmates and you tired
    of all those virgins
  begging to be branches,
fountains, marble statues.
      What red-blooded American
  boy understands girls
named Byblis, Iphis,
    Arcas? All those sisters
  spinning till their hands turned
claws, their mouths
    beaks? Arachne's nose
  falling off, then her ears, and all
for art, one more woman shriveling
    into a spider—
  maybe not the best story
for fifteen-year-olds
    even if you're prodigies
  in Latin. Medea, Medusa, Circe.
Jeez, this one's got snakes growing
    out of her head,
  this one's got dogs
where her pussy should be. Just
    what you suspected:
  women
are not what they seem.

2

One minute, a girl's in love
    with her brother, the next
  she's a faucet
that can't be turned off,
    and her brother's bathing
  in her, drinking her up. You'd think
these guys in myths would learn
    to stay away from pools
  after Actaeon was demoted
to a deer and devoured
    just for looking

down into the pond
where a goddess, who'd come to swim
                naked, was breaking
        into ripples.
It's a boy's greatest fear,
                his dogs turning on him,
        his friends hot on his trail,
tracking him down and then feasting
                on his raw flesh,
        that outrageously
out-of-control, all-night stag party.

3

Keep your trap shut.
                If there's a moral
        to the myths, it's that: blab
and you're a boulder, boast
                and one by one
        your babies are turned into toads.
Keep your wishes to yourself
                or you'll dine
        on unchewable gold;
your breasts will be wrinkled
                balloons. Don't even think
        out loud
or you'll soon end up a statue
                or a rat or a raven.
        Too late to learn from your mistakes
as you drive the family chariot
                straight
        into the sun.

4

Harder to bend than a willow,
                harder to move than a river,
        as deaf as the sea.
What do fifteen-year-olds have
                in common
        with a centaur, his long-winded
wooing of a nymph,
                simile
        heaped upon simile,
as if he could wear down the girl
                with the weight of his

elaborate tropes. Of course,
you and your friends laughed
            at a fat, bearded man
        in the body of a horse.
Like the maiden, you had your minds
            on beauty
        and what it'd be like
to be held by it,
            not something old,
        barbarically huge and sad,
and almost untranslatable.

5

Suspirar, desnudarse, sufferre.
            You're being marched
        down a candlelit marble hall,
naked, martyred, your longings
            turned elegant
        in Latin
while your coach draws diagrams
            on the board,
        his voice so serious
he could be planning the sacking
            of Troy. You're working
        on your own book
of surprises. You're a vine.
            You're dew
        on the feet of young girls,
a field of daffodils.
            Nymphs shrivel
        into nothing but a voice
out of love for you.
            Ganymede?
        Hyacinth?
How does a boy explain
            to his teammates
        he longs to be so dazzling
a god couldn't resist him?
            How does he tell his coach
        he'd like to be ethereal,
a gold-fringed bird
            with no obligations
        except to wake the world?

6

Screechings, shrills, squeaks,
       tiny, dislodged
     synonyms flinging themselves,
fur and claw, against the walls
       of your skull,
    radar gone haywire,
dislocations, near collisions,
       careenings, skiddings
    across the air.
Of course you keep silent
       when it's your turn
    to recite for the teacher.
You love Latin too much
       to trust its royal lineage
    to mucus, spit, and speech,
the nominative's obedient
       entourage: acquisitive,
    eloquently senile genitive;
supercilious dative;
       sorry-ass accusative,
    that old belly
that always gets the spear;
       and, best of all,
    the familiar
of grief and guilt, the ablative,
       always modifying,
    qualifying,
final *e*, faithful servant
       that expects nothing
    in return.

7

One moment you're ordinary,
       a son, a brother,
    and the next
a god is finding you
       so remarkable
    there's no escape
except to turn into a tree.
       And when you try to
    speak, your voice
drops. It cannot push through

                    all those thick cells
            of wood and water. Such work,
this turning, all at once, into
                    bark and leaf,
            such effort devoted
to plumbing, to making sure
                    gravity relents
            and water rises,
to digesting the sun, meal
                    after meal
            of light, your arms tired already
of the weighty obligations
                    the air is determined
            to hold you to.
Does wisteria appreciate
                    the tangle
            light gets it into?
Do clematis, ivy, morning creeper
                    feel gratitude
            for being lured up
a lattice, tricked, and left with nothing
                    more to grab onto?
            Just try to
fall to your knees, beg
                    for mercy. Kill yourself?
            Changed,
you're no more free
                    than a tree is. Like it,
            you've got responsibilities.
You've got to hold up the sky,
                    take water
            and light and air
and translate them,
                    leaf
            by leaf—into what?

Rorschach Test

It seems like a trick, the man
        pulling a card out of the deck
and placing it before the boy.
        If the boy sees a woman's groin,
it's a spider. A hand splayed out
        is a gang
dividing to get away from the cops,
        a river breaking into tributaries.
What is unmistakably a penis
        is a walking stick.
He knows he's supposed to talk
        and so he talks. The dark wings
are a boy's jacket he has spread wide
        and is trying to fly.
And that tall figure is either a tree
        or an old man watching
a girl hang from the end of a kite's tail.
        It is lifting her away,
and before she knows, she'll not be able to
        let go. It'll be no good screaming;
she'll be swept too high for anyone to hear.
        And then the doctor
puts the cards away and asks the boy what he did
        when the man loosened his belt.
Did nothing. Said nothing. Pretended
        to be too tired
to notice. He was an old man dying,
        a tree
someone was twisting a piece of fruit off,
        a branch snapped in two.
Nothing could touch him.
        Okay, imagine you are a tree now,
the doctor says, resting his hand
        on his patient's arm.
What does it feel like?
        Like nothing, the boy says.

Ovid, Book Three

The gods are so busy, so good
        at ruining lives,
we forget that
        they can't get to everyone
all at once. Fate can
        only do so much. It can't
see that absolutely all cars
        crash, all planes
slide off the runway,
        every storm
gets its chance
        at every ship.
Every village has to take its turn
        being leveled.
Every microbe must wait
        for the right opportunity
to devour a man's flesh.
        This is a tale
told often: a boy
        marked for the worst
kind of humiliation
        and spared
at the last moment.
        Out of mercy?
Perhaps. An oversight?
        Maybe. Or just boredom?
The gods get tired
        of turning men
into pigs or flowers.
        Sure, the boy was
raped, but just by a man,
        not a god,
and he let the boy go
        as no god would.

Teaching the Myth of Pelops to Ninth Graders

You'd think that if you'd been chopped up,
          boiled in a cauldron,
served up to the gods by your father, the king,
          you'd stay away
from royal dinners thereafter—that is
          if you were lucky enough
to be pieced back together.
                    The more I get caught up
with the idea, the more restless grow
          the kids. One zips
and unzips his book bag;
          another reties his shoes.
Athena just poked with her fork,
          Juno complained
that the knee joint had too much gristle,
          Hades pushed back and forth
the tongue on his plate. The penis
          was rubbery as a chicken neck
so even Aphrodite wouldn't chew it.
          It was fortunate
the gods didn't have an appetite that day.
          I look at my charges.
They're waiting for me to get to the point.
          That's a teacher's job,
in fifty minutes or less,
          to make sense
of a war, math problem, dismemberment.
          Do we ever learn?
Even Pelops' son fricasseed his brother's kids.
          The dinner table once again,
boys and girls, the seat of a family's neurosis.
          The House of Atreus
ample proof of the virtues
          of masturbation.

Why You Find So Many A's on My Class Roster

Sorry, says the mother of five, a church organist.
She didn't have time to re-type her essay.
Her husband wasn't going to let her make a fool of herself
again, he said, and so
with red pen, he'd Xed through whole paragraphs
of what she'd written, all the metaphors
that she'd delighted in,
that sounded like keys touched lightly.

Yesterday, the 7-11 clerk tore his research paper into pieces
right in front of the whole class.
La Belle Dam Sans Merci, my ass! People are starving
and you want me to redo my footnotes?

The waitress dashes in late.
Last night her apartment was broken into.
Her nine-year old called the police.
They had to take away his father in handcuffs.
Can I try the test tomorrow? she says in a rush
as if, somewhere at her back,
there's still a customer waiting.

The man with the impeccably groomed silver hair
is grateful for any class
where he's allowed to revise. His essay's not due
till next week, but he'd like to start now,
is not quite sure what's meant by critical analysis.
He's no hair stylist, he says,
but a barber. *Come by and I'll give you a trim.*
He likes having a teacher with unruly hair
and young enough to be his son.

His own boy died three years ago
of AIDS. *I didn't know he was a homo-*
sexual. He pronounces the word
as if it were one he'd just read in a book
and still had to sound out.
I didn't even know he was dying.
That's what hurt. That my son hadn't told me.
That's why I can't forgive Kevin.
He says his son's name
as if it were Latin for a rare flower
and the flower's beauty distilled in that one word.

Big Nose Relegated: The Tristia

Boohoo, boohoo, no one speaks Latin here
            and the weather's bad.
I want to come home. One more letter
            from Publius Ovidius Naso,
as if no one's ever been exiled
            before, had to learn
a new tongue, cook himself supper,
            wear a knife
to bed, laugh at others' jokes
            so he'd not be killed.
Look, we all have jobs
            and yours is
to take your punishment
            like a Roman.
His friend does not write this back.
            Instead, he lies
that he's arguing Big Nose's case
            before the emperor.
Like a spoiled child on a rainy day,
            carrying on
as if he'll be the first to die
            of nothing to do,
Publius pleads for the tides to go out
            far enough
so he might walk back to Rome.
            Bad water. Bad food.
Bad dreams. Even the disgraceful state
            of his bowels.
The old poet won't take a hint and
            shut up, all those dactyls,
elegiac couplets, futile
            attempts to figure out
exactly what went wrong
            and when.
As if a man has a right to
            go on and on
about what's happened to him,
            trying to
make sense of it all,
            and to sing
        and sing till it does.

O Beauty, Fugitive Beauty

What am I to do with all the poems
where my father had implored Beauty
to reveal herself, addressed her
gallantly like a jilted lover, rebuked her sharply?
Hundreds of heroic couplets
willed to me, a language so fired and faceted
he might have been cutting diamonds.
An ache that is buoyant fire.
Fire in my heart and head.
An ache that will never tire until I be dead.
A man imagines his affliction
a ship he is captain of, a mighty galleon
he's sailing out of the harbor
past the belly buoys at their thankless chores,
the farthest beacons,
long years, widening latitudes.
The waves may rise before him like the cliffs,
but he'll climb them;
the sky may fill with lamentations, but he will weep louder.
If the lightning throws itself in his path,
he will thrust it aside,
steer his entire crew safely home.
Suffering is a boat just large enough for one,
a patched up centerboard,
a single sail, a difficult crossing.

Aristaeus, The Son Never Talked About

One day he's humming
            to his bees,
        doing what he was born to do,
and the next day
            his hive's dead
        and he's wrestling with a weasel.
No matter what form Proteus takes,
            boar or rat
        or head full of snakes,
the boy hangs on
            till the god has no choice
        but to be wise.
Slaughter a cow a day
            and stand watch
        over the carcasses.
Aristaeus is no dummy.
            He knows cures
        often sound crazy,
so he does what he's told
            and kills cow after cow
        till on the ninth day,
out of the ninth beast's entrails,
            spills a great swarm of bees
        like books, sweat socks
moldy sandwiches from a school locker.
            To celebrate
        Aristaeus puts out trays of sugar water,
sees to the small, essential details
            of his paradise.
        A boy with honey
always on his hands?
            People expect more
        from the son of Apollo.
Not a kid with a tin ear,
            a bad case of acne,
        and no aptitude
for archery. Bees hover
            around Aristaeus
        like cats waiting to be fed.
They perch on his arms
            as if he's a shrub.

If a bee stings him
it's a compliment. Maybe
          there's courage
in not being brilliant,
in doing the same thing
          over and over,
     walking familiar grounds
and taking delight
          in what alights there.

The Suicide Note

At first it looks like a poem,
                words darkening the page
like a messenger pushing through snow,
                crossing a battlefield.
        To bring what?
A demand for surrender?
                Terms of a treaty?
        Sweet death, come swiftly!
Lines my father put down
                in his own hand
        as a teenager might—
no secretary, no typewriter now,
                just slanted letters feverishly
        rushing to their destination
as if the writer were the only one
                ever to suffer,
        words set apart on the page
as someone else might place a sculpture
                on a pedestal
        or a flowering plant by a window
so it could get the light it deserved—
                as if the best reason
        to put anything down on paper
was that you loved it—*Astrolabe, delphinium,*
                grail, solitude, frisson.
        If words couldn't
persuade a sweet, troubled man
                not to pour another whiskey,
        swallow another fistful of pills,
what were they worth? If I turn away
                from the words now
        and then turn back,
they are nomads crossing a field,
                restless, disheveled army
        of veterans, dark figures
who wandered into a clearing
                and, huddled there,
        look almost harmless,
pausing once more
                on their long migration.

From
CELL COUNT

(Texas Tech University Press, 1997)

Does Poetry Matter

American poetry belongs to a subculture. No longer part of the
mainstream of artistic and intellectual life, it has become the
specialized occupation of a relatively small and isolated group.
—Dana Gioia

I am alone.
I lie next to stone.

A man writes in the notebook he takes everywhere
in a jail, a boy really,
this shy, earnest twenty-two-year-old
who never seems comfortable
sitting—as if he's not yet used to the large, gangly body
that's grown around him.

You've got to believe me,
I never before lifted a hand to anyone. Never.

Now he goes nowhere without paper and pen,
rhymes everything. Everything
is a sonnet. He likes to hear the couplet
click shut like a door
only he has keys for. He listens for the final word,
its prompt and perfect justice.

I am alone.
I lie down next to stone.

Ratted Out

You get caught, you don't know me—
that deal sworn to as soon as the car starts,
the gun's out. *One of us gets unlucky,*
he gets amnesia. An oath
repeated, hands laid over hands.
You're my friend, you'll forget me.
        Donnie looks down
at the fist he's just made. *That's my mistake,*
all my life I've trusted people,
       he says
as if he were gazing back over decades,
not a kid nabbed only years ago
with the entire school's milk money.
       I got dimed out then too.
At first he'd stolen just enough
so one would notice.
He hid his stash on his way to the nurse.
Behind a fire extinguisher.
While every other fifth-grader was sweating out fractions,
he was on her cot, fast asleep.
       I'd have been all right
if I hadn't started pocketing more
than I could spend by myself.
       In high school
he had upped the stakes, the band's
trip money. *Shit,*
if they were dumb enough not to lock it up
in a safe, they deserved to lose it.
       I'd have got away with it too
if I hadn't let a couple of kids in
on the fun. Trust no one.
       There's no one in the world
who won't rat you out. And he looks over
at me. For the first time
in our talk, the boy looks right at me.
He does not turn away.
No one, he says.
       I mean no one.

Five to Seven, Armed Robbery

It had been one of those lazy June days
when he and his pals used to take a ball and a bat
and go to the school yard
and lie in the grass and talk about what they were going to be
someday, going to do this summer
and the next and the next.

He had thought his friends were joking
when they showed him the gun
and told him to keep his foot on the gas.
The car was in neutral
and he lounged behind the wheel.

How could he now admit he was in jail
for being stupid? He used to stand before his mirror
and wonder if he'd always be like this:
skinny and pimply,
a boy who fixed car radiators in his parents' driveway.
He'd promised his mother
soon, soon
she'd have her driveway back.
He pushes his seat away from the table,
one of those indestructible wooden school chairs
found everywhere in jail.
He goes to the window.
Well, now she has, he laughs.

Foot Soldiers

The foot won't behave.
In an interview, a council of state,
someone's shoe is always rubbing an itch
or tapping a little subversive beat
on the floor, or up
on its heel, sniffing for danger,
wary, curious,
a startled animal on its hind legs.

A foot is hard to trap for long,
always ready to escape its shoe
though it loves the sock,
the toes seeking a private darkness there.
Not many pleasures as welcome
as pulling a sock on,
the softness riding up the foot,
promising to go further, past the ankle.

In jail the prisoners wear flip-flops
like tourists at the beach,
the feet innocent
of all charges against them.
Did they twist a woman's arm behind her back
or rob a 7-11?
The hands have much to answer for.
But our feet?
Who is more oppressed and blind
than these two tired soldiers.

After he is raped,
the young man finds what comfort he can
on his cell bunk, face down, hugging his pillow,
the arch of one foot
pressing against the instep of the other,
trying to console it,
pushing down hard, sliding off,
then returning to push down harder, the right
like a clumsy hand
massaging the left, two slow-witted
brothers talking in the dark.

The Adverb

The wonder isn't that you flew into my trap,
said the spider to the fly.
The wonder is that you stayed away
so long. Surprised
to be squashed,
ant? The surprise is
you managed
in a world of leather shoes and spiked heels,
in the mad traffic of shoes,
to survive
this many days. Startled, wasp,
to be swatted in midair?
The truth is that you were lucky
not to be killed
before now. The wonder isn't
that so many newspapers fill with corpses
but that they have enough pages
for the bodies that end up inside them.
The spider feels the thread's tug.
He's hardly noticeable.
Like an adverb.
O my precious, if one thing doesn't kill you
another will. If not sooner,
then later. If not today,
then tomorrow.
Eventually.

Gaelinda

"Bitch," he said. "Shut up. I'm tired of your squirming."
I heard her telling him she was a virgin
but he just kept tugging at her sweatshirt,
pulling down her tights.
We locked her in the trunk afterwards.
"Do you want to watch?" he asked.
"Watch what," I said.
I knew. He had the gun in his hand.
He was pointing it at my face.

Even crying on the stand,
holding a handkerchief to her mouth,
she was stunning, a woman so beautiful
you'd never imagine her having to light her own cigarette
or open any door,
her eyes a dark you could sail across for days.

But she was the same person
who'd dragged a girl out of the trunk,
twisted the girl's arm behind her back.
Later we went back to the bridge
to the bushes where we'd thrown the girl.
He put another bullet in her head.
"Just in case," he said.

I can't write,
she says now and looks down at the blank page,
folds the paper neatly into smaller and smaller squares,
creasing it each time
as if she'd already said too much,
the witness stand had exhausted all the words in her.

Write about a game you played as a child
or your first bike
or the candy you couldn't live without
or the day your grandmother died
or what it was like to visit your daddy in jail,
the TV show you always watched
to make yourself feel better.
Describe a perfect day.
What'd you order at a restaurant
if you could order anything on the menu.

The lighting is bad in jail,
but we learn to work in the shadows,
the room full of whispers,
pencils saying, *yes, yes,*
yes to paper. And paper doing what it is supposed to do,
Not bothered by misspellings,
profanity, lies,
not holding our bad handwriting against us,
letters like dark, stubborn dwarfs
or squashed insects
or the veins of a gnawed leaf
or the scrawl water leaves in the sand of creek beds,
old angers, hungers, stories told before
that will be told again.
The paper takes it all down.

A Place for Sorrow

What if we set a place at the table
for Sorrow, let everyone take a turn there
and be fed delicacies,
the best portion,
the part of the slaughtered beast saved
for the boy who tries to rip his hair from his scalp,
the daughter who scars her perfect face.
What if we honored even the lesser gods?
Discord. Discontent.
Ennui. The household deities
Worry, Remorse, Rancor, Self-pity?
What if from birth boys were expected
to grip windowsills, sob inconsolably,
even their breathing a question
of faith, girls trained to be restless,
to go without sleep,
to pick up a book and put it down, dial a phone
and hang up as soon
as their call is answered, a whole corps
of children schooled in the fine arts
of being disenchanted and distraught,
their lips parched
even though they'd just drunk the sweetest fruit?
Right after they'd feast, they'd open their mouths wide
like baby birds, complain
of the loneliness just after being kissed.
At the edge of losing their voices they'd raise them
in dirges, lamentations, groans, wheezing,
deep coughs, as if this time maybe
the mouth might spit out its great wad of misery,
the throat pull up all of the body's darkness
and be done with it.
Who else but the desperate
would wrench a song out of something so out of tune
even after they've given up all belief in the efficacy of song,
the air pressed out of them,
all that's left them
the blood's tried measures?

What if they were welcome at all great occasions,
inaugurations, weddings, funerals, baptisms?
Invited to offer a few words,
they'd sing.
It would be a song painful to hear,
and everyone would listen.

Sudden Draft

Richie finally begins talking about what matters
to him, the pencil box he had as a kid,
the way the piano seemed to rise to his fingers,
push against them—*almost like a cat,*
he says, *like all it wanted me to do was pet it—*
and how he couldn't make his hands press down on the keys
after his brother died; it seemed wrong
even to hum in the house,
to shape his mouth into words—
there was nothing worth saying anymore.

He's shivering as if a wind had slipped past one iron door
and then another, shoved its way
this far into jail,
and just now he's felt it on his neck.

There is a clear detergent smell on the tables
and a leaf on the floor.
How did it get there?
Richie picks it up and studies it
like a clue that has something to teach him
if he just looks long enough.

None of us talks straight when the girls are in class.
Have you noticed?

Old Mr. Mac stops coughing.
Stephen glances up from his science fiction comic book.

None of us. We've got too many Jaguars
and Porsches zooming around the room.
We're too busy spending all those millions we've stashed.
Richie looks up.
He's said something he hadn't expected to
and it's too late to take it back.

And then Sly's nodding,
Tiny's giving the *right on* sign,
and even the Ice Man tires of twisting his shirttail
into tighter and tighter knots
and wheels his chair over
and pounds on the table, *Motherfucking right!*
The rookie's got a point, you know.

And then Richie's blushing—
that look a kid gets
when he's said something worth an adult paying attention,
someone much older than he is
finding him capable, important—

one of those moments that hush the voice,
soften a face
that's tried all week to look like stone,
like iron, a transformation
that, even if it doesn't alter anything in a man's life,
for a few seconds
alters everything.

Sidereal Time

Why have I given him this watch?
What appointments does he have to keep in jail?
Lifting its scratched bubble face,
its little coolness to his cheek,
he tells me about his first watch, a Bulova
lifted off his stepfather's bureau,
the first thing he'd ever stolen.
Not till he climbed the railroad bridge
had he slipped it on.
As he talks, the guards come closer
as if they can tell from his head's tilt,
his hand's trembling,
he's about to start something
only they can finish.
That's the worst part of being in jail, he says,
there's no good place to hide.
At home he could run away, scale a bridge,
put hundreds of feet of air
between him and everyone who could hurt him.
Maybe he'd never go home.
Maybe he'd stay up there, sleeping with the winds
and the ghosts of trains.
This watch I've given him isn't so different
from his old one. It's luminescent too.
He cups his palm over it.
Together we peer into the darkness
he's made with his hands.
There are tiny beams radiating out
like those when you shut your eyes tight,
the kind of light you imagine
stars really make.
He could strap it to his wrist
and wear it past one iron gate
and then another.

From
THE ONE TRUE RELIGION

(Quarterly Review of Literature, 1997)

The Flood

We wait for the hired woman
to shut her door and then
her light, and then the house itself
grows quiet as a ship that's turned off its engines.
Everywhere that isn't desk or bureau or chair
is ocean, a flood spreading as far
as we can see. Capsized,
we clutch the sides of our beds.
Wave after wave strikes us, tries to
drag us away. *Don't*
let go, you whisper. If I do
there'll be no way
you can save me. My fingers hurt from grasping
yours. My body's too great a weight
for anyone to lift. If it wants to fall
that badly, maybe
I ought to let it. I can't
hold on forever, can I?
Yes, you whisper.
The word reaches down into the darkness
where I dangle.
Yes, you can. It is a command.

The One True Religion

1

One talking, one listening,
one asking questions so the other would not stop.
Did she appear in a vision to the older boy
or to the younger? *Fighting Pehbee,*
a goddess as distracted and angry as the weather.
This was how they played on their way home from school,
making supper by themselves,
keeping the same story going for weeks:
to turn the rain on the roof into arrows,
shadows into dogs sleeping at their feet,
each day's terror—ordinary beatings,
doors slammed, a house in ruins—changed
at night into glorious acts, a fortress
under siege. Their mother had been shoved
to the ground, held there
by a man they'd never seen before,
a man who had brushed them aside
like branches in his way.
He had a needle, a black bag.
Their father had watched
as if someone was holding his arms.
Do something! they begged their mother.
Make the man stop!

2

Thus the last daughter of Brem escaped
north, past the tribes covered in fur,
people whose breath melts ice.
And when finally she was too chilled and weary
to journey further, she lay down
in a field and slept for three days and woke
to see before her a statue so real
at first she mistook it for the goddess.
She could hear the winds cry from the stone mouth.
And when it was morning she looked down,
and though she had not realized she'd been great with child,
she saw now that she had given birth
to two sons: he who would become Jeren Rother,
he who would be Rowal, keeper of the sacred spring.
And the first word on their lips
was the name of the goddess.

3

Even now the two boys crawl up to the attic,
sky so black through the narrow window
it's easy to forget they're in a house,
on a street, in a town,
and the darkness draws them toward it
as they chant, *Pehbee, Pehbee,*
not so she can hear and come back,
but for the watery sounds rubbing on stones,
sharp jagged rocks
dangerously smoothed.

A Way to Pass the Time

The strangulations and poisonings began
as a means of filling the empty moments
in the doctor's waiting room
or in the backseat on the way home.
We'd hijack a plane or kidnap a baby,
and one more afternoon would pass in rescue
and revenge. Especially good at germ warfare,
we spread contagion differently
each time, so it'd be harder
to find a cure. What was a day
without danger, a little calculated
cruelty to overcome? *Let's play,* we'd say,
and it would take all morning to get out the maps,
draw up the treaties we'd eventually break,
mark off new boundaries, swap secret powers.
It was hard work being both hero and bad guy,
a civil service of villains.
A simple assassination plot demanded passports,
a portfolio of documents.
We surveyed the land, studied blueprints,
the exact measurements for where to plant a bomb,
what exits to block off.
No one appreciates how much effort is required
to blow up a skyscraper or burn a village
or enslave a population. Soon it wasn't enough
to invade a country. We had to
build roads there, establish a postal service,
set up a banking system,
teach the people to love the very army
that had seized their homes.
Even before we'd conquered one planet
we were already building rockets
to subdue another. Go to school?
Whom could we trust
in our absence to see the poor were fed,
the rivers dammed, justice done?
We had obligations now, a bureaucracy
to see to, a world
that could not do without us.

How the Thavigeans Say the World Began

In the beginning there was light
and there was darkness
and the dark loved the light
as a glutton loves the feast set before him,
as a tidal wave relishes the village it's about to devour,
as the knife admires the pale throat
it intends to slit. Out of the dark
were created men, shadows
like waves that refused to fall
back into the great watery mass we know as darkness now,
and because these men were the first
they were free to name everything
that came afterwards: their children, the weather,
the changing of the light, flowers
and birds. They decided what sound to fasten
to what shapes; for example
which winged, pollen-sipping creatures to call
vermin, which to imagine lovely,
what to hate, what to hoard,
what to spit out, what to savor.
These first men were no different from any
who followed: they raised armies,
built walls around their cities,
and over their towers and on their masts
hoisted flags. Everything dark
they hid. They painted in the color of light
on water, light
on a field of wheat. The halls of the palace.
The stadium. The baths. The pawnshops.
Even the prisons.
But under everything they knew
lay darkness. Even their language, each word
created out of darkness. Deceit,
ruins. Perhaps light was not meant to rule the earth,
to preside in courts. Evening
after evening, it gave up its throne,
wilted, let its empire be eaten away.

Two Boys Are Talking

One has wrapped a quilt around himself.
It fans out at his feet like the folds of a great dress.
The other has fallen to his knees
on a rock so wide and flat
it appears to be a perfect spot for sacrifice.
In the stone there's a small dark pool of rainwater.

These are tears.
Drink them, the older brother says.
Drink them all.
He lets go of the weaker one's wrist.

Someone has to pay.
Someone must die.
He picks up a knife,
rubs it against rock to sharpen it,
drags it lightly down the younger boy's arm,
presses it to his abdomen.
He leans over his brother
like a doctor explaining each step of a difficult operation.

He's so close to him
he could be whispering into his ear.
He could be tucking him into bed.

The point is for both to believe
the one might actually push the knife in,
the other really feel the blade enter,
a pain so deep he could never recover.

If You Are Nine

You stop and consider
never moving from the spot you've chosen
as being far enough
from where you left and safer
than where you are headed.
Sometimes you are a warrior,
sometimes an outlaw
whose renegade band would gladly die by his side.
Bring me the tyrant's head!
you shout to the trees.
Sometimes you're an old man telling his secrets
to the few who bend over his deathbed,
those who must carry on his work.
Or you are a scientist
and the planet is about to collide with another planet
and you are the only one
with the power to change the earth's axis.
But sometimes you're just a child and trembling
from the cold and too scared to go back
and too scared to go forward.
The rain's under your collar
again, it keeps finding
the exact same spot on your neck
no matter how tight you pull your coat.
Count on this: the passage of time
solves nothing. The temperature will keep
dropping. The closer it gets to zero
the less use the night has
for anything human, anything that hopes
to make a stand. The world stretches apart
till you wonder how anyone crosses even the smallest
distance, say between this stretch of shadows
and that spiked clump of bushes,
this burned out streetlight and that dark
judgmental oak. *You've got to get moving*
you say to yourself. *Now.*
Do you want to stay in one place
all your life? You do
and you don't.

Look Down! See Those Rocks? That's Brem

You wanted to play Brem?
your brother teases. *Well, let's play.*
He unbuttons your shirt,
starts to loosen your belt.
The rain has stopped.
The clouds have sailed away,
ships heading somewhere else,
leaving the harbor empty,
dark, the sky
as close as any kingdom the two of you ever made up
and as huge. You pull free
from your brother's hands. He lets go
as if you were a doll
that'd just come alive.
For once it's you scaring him.
Still out of breath from the climb up,
you lean out the lighthouse window.
Here's your chance to walk on air.
It may be your last.
And look, there's a path
as if it'd always been there
and now you're just noticing it.
One of those moments dreamed of so often
when it happens, you almost believe you've caused it,
mist and moonlight
laying down mother of pearl.
You'd gone back and forth between worlds
so many times, there had to be a bridge,
and now you're going to cross it
alone if you must.
Make the moon appear
and you make the mist solid.
You've got your clothes all the way off now.
It'd be so easy to step on this path
like walking on atoms
shifting, opalescent
light that looks as if it could hold no one
and yet it is so lovely it seems a failure in you
not to trust your feet to it, the pull
of every story, places too dark even for the one telling it
to describe.

Career Counseling

You can be whatever you set your mind to,
teachers are fond of saying.
Sit down, son, the career counselor points to a chair,
pulling out brochures like a travel agent.
Where are you headed?
As if no destination were out of the realm of possibilities.
He just has to plug it into the computer,
check flights, book tickets far enough in advance.
You can be whatever you wish,
a boy's father says, meaning lawyer, teacher,
engineer, M.D., R.N., C.P.A.,
speaking in that voice parents use, knowing
they're being more understanding
than their parents ever were. *Tell me,*
what do you really want to do?

What can the boy say? *I want to be a child*
adopted by vultures. Or a blind girl
who lives in a cave. Or a hermit who speaks to lizards.
He wants to be washed up,
a castaway, searching for the crew he's been separated from,
shipwrecked on this planet, marooned in a human body.
Maybe that's why he touches himself so often—
to see if he can feel a fragment
of who he really is, a piece of light broken
off from a star he's spent so much energy trying to get back to.
Maybe that's why he lights matches
and presses the flames into his palms
as if pain holds the answer
folded up in its petals. Maybe the only way back
is to hurt, to rub against shattered glass.

What's on your mind?
asks the doctor. *Don't be afraid. You can tell me*
anything. The boy is thinking
of what he'll have to give up if he opens his mouth,
what every young man or woman
serious about making a living has to:
gazing at leaves, their elegant distractions,
or the creek's long run-on sentences,
its exclamations, its parentheses, its tireless questions.

What if we made graduation a little more honest,
conducted a ceremony
where every eighteen-year-old dragged onto the field
all he'd hidden in his closets,
all she'd loved but had no excuse to hold onto?
Final exams would require every student
to write down the idle thoughts
she'd sworn never to think again.
Fire would grade the papers
and everyone would get the same mark,
flames correcting the notebooks
filled with spaceships or Greek gods
or imaginary solar systems, words that excited a boy
or girl just to put them on paper: *wastrel,*
changeling, crucible, relic, galaxy,
maelstrom, cataclysm.

Sit down, son.
Tell me what you want to do with the rest of your life.

From
PLACES OF COMFORT, PLACES OF JUSTICE

(Humanities and Arts Press, 1988)

Crewcut

Just before I was arrested
I remember thinking I should get a haircut,
and needing something to focus on besides the sirens,
I closed my eyes and imagined the scissors, a silvery bird
pecking at me. I was an old nest
it was tidying, a thicket it was picking at for sweet bugs.
The scissors moved in the air just above me.

I remember crewcuts.
My mother made me and my brothers get them.
We loved the moment just after
running our hands across the bristles,
all those hairs at military attention.
Then, older, we'd ask for more:
the barber would rub stickum at the front tip,
bestow a slight curl.
That was the only place we needed to rub a comb through,
and we combed and combed,
glad to have something a bit stylish about us,
a reason to look in the mirror.
We'd come from a haircut
as if nothing in the world could beat us,
we were that sweet-smelling,
that sharp, as if bringing home something special
to show our mother, a treat.
And now I imagine how my mother would've felt
if she'd been here to see me lie down
on a street still damp from the rain.
She'd have been almost as concerned about my long hair
as about my being arrested,
as if both rebellions would lead to trouble too foreign
for her to protect me from.

A few old women, several middle-aged men, and some college kids,
we were trying to stop jeeps and trucks
with their dangerous cargoes.
We must've looked a raggedy row of bodies,
like pictures of dead fowl laid out
for sportsmen magazines to show how good the kill was.
Occasionally the wind lifted a scarf or coat flap
like a loose feather. We'd been waiting for so long

we found ourselves almost hoping for the gas,
the clubs, the handcuffs.

In this county jail for the third time in his life
my cellmate—twenty-two, here for petty theft—
frets with his hair. He's trying to keep it feathered,
can't stop it from flying off his forehead
like some broken wing that won't stay down.
Everyone can see he's damaged, knows
to peck at him. His mother has just died.
One of the guards, seeing his head hung down,
thinking he's just another kid back from trial,
just another prisoner to be shipped from here,
laughs, pokes at his chest,
Hey, Ferris, you look as if your old lady's
been screwing behind your back.

Yeh, and yours fucks ducks.
That's all he has left, these insults, wet matches
he keeps trying to strike.
He pushes his hands now through his thick hair
and makes both sides lift,
black, straggly wings. For safety's sake
he's given up showering, shampooing,
combing out the gnarls.
If they're going to treat you like a criminal,
you might as well look like one.
And I think of my mother—dead now like Ferris's—
who knowing how little she could keep me safe
put so much emphasis on a trim haircut,
well-groomed nails,
took such pleasure trimming her son's clean and perfect.

Today in the barber shop
I know why my cellmate is crying.
It's unfair to have women here
in jail, especially one bringing in her scissors
and combs, on her day off showing up here
to teach the inmate trainees how to give men a little style,
leaning over Ferris now, touching his neck,
cutting away the knotted curls of his raggedy hair.
Your mother is dead
and this is the only gift you know to give her.

Secret Gifts

Is your Dad in jail still? Nora's teacher
had called across the room and the class had laughed.
Before I left home,
my daughter sat me down and warned me:
I was to behave this time.
I was not to get arrested.

And now we've taken the courthouse over.
None of us had believed the gas
till we gagged from it. One of the police
had grabbed a boy by his sweater,
another brought down a club on the kid's skull
as we tore him away. A hundred of us have made it inside,
guards set at the doors,
small groups of us telling the stories of our injuries over and over
as if somehow those who'd hurt us
might hear, like parents in another room
looking down at their guilty hands.

Do you always have to get your name in the paper?
Nora wants me to be nothing but a father.
one who expects good grades,
rides bikes with her when her friends aren't around,
lets her tease and comb
the snarls out of his dark, matted hair.
But here, waiting for the police to be sent in,
I find deep in my pockets
mints with sour jellies in their middles,
cashews, raisins she must've hidden in the good jacket
I always wear to get arrested—two
store-bought cookies, hers and my favorites.
As she'd do, I loosen the sugar with my nails,
raise each crystal to the light.
It's a small magnificence.

Even the crumbs will do,
and I begin searching the seams, along the threads,
into the sugary silt of my coat,
wetting my fingertips,
lifting to my tongue the dust of peppermint,
taste of salt.

The Medical Center for the Aging

Today I teach the class about metaphor.
Imagine you have wings, I tell them, *feathers.*
Lift, I whisper to Dr. Fernald,
to the retired headmistress Eve Briscoe,
to the frail pianist Eleanor Conwyn, to Idwell Robinson,
who, in 1913, was champion of all the British Isles.
Where is the wind carrying you?
What do you see below?
I stand behind Mr. Paxton, rub his shoulders.
Imagine wings there,
you are soaring. How does it feel?
Scared, Isabel Pfeiffer says,
who once raised millions for a young ladies' academy.
Embarrassed, Professor Railsback adds.
Why swimming? I've always loved swimming,
replies Mrs. Behn, because she answers that to everything.
Nervous, insecure, apprehensive, lonely,
come other shy responses. *No, no exhilarated!*
insists Mrs. Carduso. *I'm rising.*
This is how wide my wingspan is,
she laughs, spreading out her arms.
I'm casting shadows on everyone,
little children are scared at first,
they think I'm some sort of prehistoric bird
escaped from a museum. We fly over mountains,
rivers, veer off to each person's home.
I make each name the town. We go by Santa Fe,
Topeka, Sioux City, Springfield, Des Moines,
then float back over Doylestown
and circle the Medical Center
where the doctors and nurses rush out, gazing up,
pointing their shaking fingers.
Be reasonable. Come down. Come down this very instant.
But Mrs. Carduso wants to fly on,
straight into the sun, to get so close to the source of light
it singes her feathers, and then to plummet.
She catches my arm
tightly and I almost cry out, her fingernails pressing
through the sleeves into my skin,
but I make myself not flinch.

I hold onto the pain. She's got me dangling
over the earth. I can see how far I'd fall
if she were to loosen her grip.

Shit

Damn it to hell,
my father roamed the house, Sundays, looking for a hammer.
On the seventh day he couldn't rest
but had to fix things. *Damn*
was the word grown-ups were supposed to use
if they swore in front of kids.
Bitch, bitch, that's all my boss ever does.
My brother was allowed to use the verb.
It seemed like an old jalopy he'd bought with his own money,
had souped up. It left gravel spinning.
Bitch. I whispered the word so often to myself,
once it slipped out at the dinner table
and I was slapped, was righteously indignant.

It was a dog, only a dog I meant,
Mother. It was you,
I said under my breath. How did everything turn crazy on me
all at once, my parents' voices harsh,
accusing. Everyone wanted something from me
I couldn't give, they'd no right to keep me at home
and go on demanding it of me.
Assholes, cunts.
Cunt was the word of someone who'd just as soon kill a person
as go for a ride. *Fuck them all.*
Fuck. How at seventeen had I lived without such a word?
Like a car only I had the keys for in the house.
Fucking shit.

I can almost pinpoint the day I began to depend
on this last curse. *Shit,* I'd say,
waking to the baby's cry, and it'd actually be shit,
sweet, clayey. I'd peel it off her bottom.
Now my daughter is eleven and moody as a candle,
as alert, a paradox of tallow
and flame, melting and burning. Hurt in school,
she's pulled all her blankets off her bed
and cried herself to sleep on the floor.
And in class today a student not much older than Nora
tells us how she leads her younger sisters into a closet
and plays them U-2 and Platinum Blonde and Shelia E,
gets them to sing along

so they don't hear the full impact
of their mother's head against the wall, their father's
slamming it there again, again.

Then a boy's talking, he says it's his fault
his brother died, he hadn't told his parents about the tapes
he'd overheard, he'd been sworn by his brother
to say nothing of the needle
he'd found in the drawer. *Shit.*
By the windowsill a boy is rubbing his forehead hard,
to the left a girl is looking away.
Shit. Not as in: *I'm not going to take anymore of your shit.*
Not as in: *I don't give a shit.*
But *Shit*—like when there's a sob in your throat
and there are kids actually crying in the room
and you don't know how you're going to go on teaching
if the students are going to be this honest, this tender,
and the moment's so beautiful and scary
you have to fuck it up.

Prayer

God of the feather rubbed across a cheek,
God of the tuft of fur under a cat's chin,
cluck of tongue making hoofbeats, all
brisk, clear sounds listened for
that fit the ear, folds and wrinkles,
God of lucky alignments,
God of the condom a thirteen-year-old
rolls and unrolls on his thumb.

God of bevel and slide rule, tongue and groove,
slipknot, paperclip, the bolt's threads—
God of pipes and plugs, tumblers in a lock.

It feels like a nail is being driven into
my skull, she cried out.
Then a gentle woman's brain is dead,
then her body too—
death fitting tight as those middle years of marriage,
as the ring she tugged at, pushed against
the hard bone of her knuckle.
We stand at the grave
and try to make our feet fill the prints dried there.

Surely there is no god of pain and disease,
only some lesser, propitiatory one
we can pray to. God of nut and bolt,
safety pin and rubber band, God of latch and key,
sleeve and gentle tugging there,
God of the hand on an inner arm,
God of a whispered urgency, two friends at a table
talking over the sound of rain,
God of long vowels that linger in our mouths,
whose look we've come to love:
moon, piano, spider, sieve. A language
that is often just a solace to say,
cinnamon and *orange, seam* and *wrinkle.*

God of such beautiful approximations,
a saying *yes,* that will have to do,
to see it, feel it. *Yes,*
that will do.

From
THE WAY WATER RUBS STONE

(The Word Works, 1987)

Dorks, Nerds, Wimps

Words spit out, chosen
for their ugliness, sounding like bad-tasting vegetables,
roots you'd feed to pigs,
food only the hungry would eat.
Geeks, my oldest boy whispers,
meaning the rids from the district's other high school,
rah-rahs, bandos,
wanting them to overhear,
to make out the words his lips form.
Nerd, his younger brother says
as we pass a boy on a bike;
he means any kid who wears plaid, has glasses, rides alone,
his mouth open as if swallowing,
as if the air's rushing in, as if there were air all inside him.
My children laugh when I tell them
how in fifth grade I was voted best girl.
My sons howl in delight, knowing
they're nothing like their father,
they're in no danger of being elected that.
I remember what it's like to decide
somebody else has to be the *dickface* now, the *faggot.*
In ninth grade, moving to a new town,
I had the chance at last to shout *asshole,*
shithead from my new friends' cars
as we peeled away. *A nobody.*
A nothing. That's what we called boys
who looked off into the distance,
who fingered change in their pockets.
The kids who *took up space.*
At seventeen I was always afraid of being found out.
What if a kid showed up from the old school?
Kippy playing football? Class vice-president?
You've got to be kidding. The same Kippy
who got a boner in the shower-room,
the one who flunked shop,
that jerk-off, momma's boy, moss teeth?
Some boys fling a word at another boy
and run away, drive away. It doesn't matter the age.
The word is left there
as if meant for him only, a magic stone.
Chances are he will pick it up, rub it,
it seems, forever.

Farts

Fifty-six in an hour, the boys tell me
when I pick them up after their week away,
maybe only one or two from the world's best.
Fifty-six in one room
with five boys—like a sixth-grade math problem:
If each boy expels gas every third minute
how long will it take
to fill a room with their smell?—
with Big Bertha, the A Bomb, the Guided Missile.
They have names for each fart, doing this for the record,
for the room's honor,
for the camp's.
What would the child-rearing books advise?
Why, son, you must feel quite proud of yourself.
But how about putting that effort
into something a little more constructive now?
Really I'm feeling admiration
for these twelve-year-olds, a respect
probably better not expressed
to my son or his friends. Who doesn't
remember as a child
at least once or twice sliding his hand down
into the crack of the buttocks? Admit
there were times
you purposely broke wind, pushing air
up through the bathwater, a few fat bubbles,
then a trail of tiny ones like from a diver's mask,
a kind of play rarely talked about.
There's a certain decorum involved here.
Just after the last of his friends is left off,
my son tells me he's been waiting a long time
to take a crap,
to sit on a toilet his alone,
this same boy who at two years old,
while I shaved, used to squat beside me
and with fierce pride squeeze out each stool,
the sweet enormity
of the smell filling the room, reaching
into its every corner.

Now he locks the door on us all,
taking over the bathroom
with a pile of comic books and the sports page.
His family will have to wait,
a week if necessary. For days he'd held in
what's dark and his
till he could be alone, bent over, the light
on the toilet's water reflecting the lobes
of his buttocks. What if each of us were disgusted
by our own mucus, saliva, the goat of our armpits,
if we couldn't stand our own smells,
to have them exotic on our fingertips?
Isn't this so like us humans:
so eager to show off,
so private, lifting a whiff of earth,
odor of warm rain,
alien, ancient fragrances, the body's wind?

Ice Fishing

For hours at this hole in the ice
the boy pretended to be the one person alive
left with the task of testing the world's depths,
pulling up line, measuring by arm's lengths,
feeling the little tug
of the metal weight, then the lovely looseness
of the line. This morning he'd heard his mother breaking dishes,
his father sobbing with anger again,
crying out, *For God's sake,*
for God's sake, Kit!
He thought if he just tried hard enough,
did one thing well,
he might fix things. He'd bring home a fish
just as if he were a normal kid in a normal family,
and his mother would be so pleased she'd get dressed,
and the kitchen would fill with tarragon and butter
and fish sizzling, that luxurious oily smell,
and his father would open the windows at last,
and the winter air, sharp and clean,
would cut through the grease
of too much happiness.

Trial and Error

It's not even been a week since the operation.
Most of my body is water,
like a planet, so it'll take a while to exhaust me
of all life-bearing seed.
Because I love this boy undressing by the creek,
his helpless, foolish belly,
his small buttocks,
my three-year-old daughter's toes, so white and huge
underwater she cries out in delight,
I imagine one more child
conceived just before the last sperm swims free.
At night, when my wife touches me,
I almost believe the dark universe is flowing
under me, around me,
and I am lifting with its high tide
like that small, perfect ship, Eden, rigged
and set afloat in time.
I am riding with a wave to its crest.
I've never understood why the God of the Bible
proved so impatient with Adam.
I want a stowaway, a mistake,
another son or daughter,
a child with thin wrists and weak eyes
and surprising strength
in the ankles, a fast runner,
a girl or boy so beautiful I might trust again
in her immortality, in his. Unlike God,
with none of His premeditated designs on the world,
His permanent dissatisfactions,
I'd welcome a little carelessness in a son,
a daughter's wild curiosity,
these children tearful and stubborn after falling,
this recklessness
that returns them over and over
to one more brave try.

Like All the Other Geeks

He's the only one of his friends home Saturday night,
like all the other geeks, he says,
without a date. *You know nothing!*
he screams at you. Try to comfort him
and he'll sit closer to the television,
he'll turn it up
as if it were the only reasonable thing in the house.
This is how the rest of his life will be: dull,
dull. He's convinced of that.
At 3 a.m., hearing him push upstairs at last,
you try to get back to sleep
like how many fathers or mothers imagining
the brave speeches they'll make the next day
to their children, the exact words
worked out in the dark, deep convictions
that once you're out of bed
seem beyond your powers? Nothing
you say to your son will equal this ardent love
that swells you, driving to work,
taking out the trash,
rehearsing the quiet interrogation you'll make,
jokes to underplay each question,
trying not to probe, not to scare him off.
Admitting too much, how could a boy dress for school,
wait with the others at the bus stop,
get through lunch?
You try to remember the month, the week
your life together changed,
as if fixing the precise date and time
you could have it back, rainy days
with the two of you pushing open doors, shutters
in cardboard boxes, using scissors like a knife,
teasing each other, those risks you could afford then,
the wrong cuts. Your boy loved to stab
in as many places as possible,
see how much light his house could take,
vistas of sea, of mountains,
five or six more openings than most walls could bear.
You'll ruin it, you'd warned him, you'd begged—
this the most splendid of houses he'd made.

Couldn't he save just this one.
But no, he laughed, grabbed the scissors
from behind your back.
More doors! More windows everywhere!

Maybe You Should Try Something Else for a While

Why depend on any one thing?
a wise counselor suggested.
Why not just enjoy the sun on your arms,
the back of your neck? Why lock yourself in a room
of shadows and write about the light?
Ever since I was a boy, I needed something mysterious
to return to. I'd sewn wings
out of all the feathers I collected,
each stitch hidden so that nothing of my human hand
showed. I used to stand at the attic window
wearing nothing but quills
and think so hard that, opening my eyes,
I'd be surprised I wasn't flying.

And now here I am again, high above the house,
in a room whose door I'm careful to shut.
When my youngest son comes up looking for toys—
lead soldiers, puppets—
for when I'm ready to go back to playing with him,
I put my hand over the words I've just written,
that old reflex. How would a kid explain a father
who strapped wings to himself?
How does a girl kiss her date goodnight
if from an upstairs window comes the moaning
of a father rocking back and forth
as he types, like some blind singer
on his piano, trying to get the house to lift off the ground.
What children don't want their parents to behave,
to do only what they understand?

Aren't we enough? my wife asks
when I mope after coming down from the attic.
And when I kiss her,
does she breathe in the feathers,
notice the tiny, white scratches left on her arms?
But who doesn't want one's hours alone—
at a piano, on the computer,
the inventions one whispers over—
to add up to something?

As a kid I'd go off by myself to a pond
and climb the highest rock, undress, and stand there
trying to get the courage to dive again.
I made myself look down

till it seemed I mattered to the water below,
to the sky in it. It was all glimmerings.
It hurt not to be inside those waves of light.
Isn't that how longing often feels?

Just once, even if it's crazy to hope for,
we want this hoarded lightness,
our ingenious devices to work,
to find ourselves soaring,
wings carrying us into the world.

Shooting Baskets

The boy pries up the ice from the driveway
till there's blacktop and he's shooting
with one eye on the rim,
one on the window above him, the lamp there.
No, he doesn't really expect his Dad to put down his paper,
that tired, shy man, to come out into such cold,
or even to look down, wave.
But the dribble of a basketball
is the sound of a boy who won't give up,
who believes that if you perform the same act over and over
something wonderful happens.
In his games he starts hopelessly behind—
45-7, 62-13, 74-22—
and at halftime kneels, draws shadow plays
on the little ice left. He's ashamed of the whole team;
how can they look anyone in the eyes after this?
And then it's all two-handed set shots
from behind the trash barrels, sky hooks at garden's edge,
a fast break started at a snowdrift
and ending with his crashing
against the garage doors, the sag there
a kind of belly from where he's flung himself
many times before. Taking his own pass,
he dribbles around ice patches,
one long stride into the air and across,
and he's floating again towards the basket
as if he might lift like a curve forever,
his hand following the ball's arc, reaching
after what he just let go. Each evening he listens
for that moment the ball drops
perfectly—not rolling around the rim and
rocking out, not even banked
off the backboard, but falling with the pure justice
he's waited for, the pleasure
of hearing—no, actually feeling—
from fifteen feet out, from thirty, in his fingertips
the swish, the ball jostling the strings.
It's that kind of sudden rightness,
an acknowledgement, and he wants it
once more, and in the little fragment of light
his father's lamp casts down
he shoots again and again and again.

From
MAKING WINGS

(State Street Press, 1983)

PLACE OF RESIDENCE

(Sparrow Press, 1983)

LITTLE HARBOR

(Quarterly Review, 1984)

Making Wings

We hunt up little kids to scare with the wings
we've sewn from our grandfathers' Hawaiian shirts,
our mothers' black silk gowns,
eyes stitched onto darkness,
huge red tongues flickering from under our arms.
Six of us jumble in the attic heat,
clinging like bugs,
so outside we can run damp and individual
with a breeze dividing us
as we fly our costumes over the yard,
grip both sides of a coat,
and spread them wide,
swooping down from garage or back porch.
Clear plastic cleaves to our elbows,
finds our most intimate places:
the fat at the back of our legs, our knees' hollows, ankle hair.
We pluck the Saran Wrap off like an old embarrassment,
push ourselves before a wind,
and finally are lifting with it.
In the evening we fasten nail files and sandpaper
to our wings so they'll be as shrill
or sad as we wish
and signal from lilac to forsythia, from oak to toolshed.
When the rest of us are called in,
one keeps his wings on and causes them to sing
and sing like an insect in the dusk
for the simple delight of it,
for the quick, busy pleasure
of making music spring out of his own body.

The Man at the Upstairs Window

When I was eight and slept two flights up,
one night
all night a man watched outside my window,
his chin on the sill,
his eyes on the soft part of my skull,
his body stiff
as if to show he was no father or father's friend,
but a more patient man.
I did not dare turn on my stomach to face him,
lift my fingers off the sheet,
brush the glass between us. He flickered there
like a candle I could not blow out.

By daybreak
I knew something no one else in the house did.

Correspondence

Some nights in bed my brother wakes me
and tells me his dreams
and makes me repeat them before I may close my eyes
again. *When you fall sleep, Kip,*
dream what I did, dream it with me.

On Saturday afternoons, Timothy makes me undress
and lie under the covers,
a letter he's just written slipped up my right sleeve
to deliver, another up my left
to bring back. *Now dream!* he says.

We enter our naps with gifts for his dream lords:
a weeping bowl, a bronze feather.
We go dressed in the silks stolen from our mother;
our father's long robes we wear to be generous.
Timothy demands I kiss the hem of each.

When he wakes, his face stiffens into its familiar angers.
The hooded men have just let him go
and he gazes from their light
into ours. I pretend I have been dreaming too
and make up stories about the splendor I witnessed.

The dust of jewels is on Timothy's fingers.
I wish I could believe the words he has entrusted
to my care, the strange watery syllables
he has arranged for me to return with,
and though I do not understand them,

as soon as they are on my tongue
and my brother is translating them
once again,
I welcome the blessings they bestow,
heed the warnings I bring back from the other world.

Home Alone

Taka tajarranda kinder
asktha sith,
kadooun takesehir a Brem.

The music of a boy by himself.

Let the mind worry about meaning
and not the mouth.

A boy sings his true song alone.

The Little We Are Entitled To

We practice begging between beds.

You are Lord Hunger,
I am Bread.
What is placed in my hand shall be
placed in yours.

Splendid, splendid.
You show me how
to bow pathetically, to stumble and faint,
to make my throat so dry
each word is a gasp.

Be the Earl of Infinite Zeroes.
I am your man,
the obsequious Decimal.

This Morning's Mail

The boy arranges his china animals in the cool
part of the rug just before the front door
so he can hear the mailman's hands,
the envelopes' whispers,
the metal mail slot's little clanging exclamation.
He wants to brush against a man
without the man's knowing,

to be a part of the great business of men,
and what better way than by gathering his father's letters,
gazing into the steamy windows
of the bills—imagining exotic dangers
inside the soft blue air-mail his father will unfold,
vague warnings
within the envelopes with no return address?

Messages from many nations arrive,
and he is at the center of his father's world
to receive them long before his father does.
He's already emptied the wastebasket
of its ashes and tissue
so the envelopes might fall into a clean darkness
and be his again, almost

straight from his father's hands.
Sometimes a child sees his whole life's pattern
suddenly in the light scattered
on a rug. He hears a man's hands on the door's other side
and suspects this is how to love a man:
without a man's knowledge,
touching what the man has touched.

Chores

1

You'll have to do this in the army,
my mother liked to shout from her ironing.
Now ten years after the war I quietly evaded,
I teach my son to put away his clothes,
instruct him in how to give his bed a military tuck,
how to snap the wrinkles out of his pants,
roll one sock into another,
a whole basketful all his to match and marry off.

2

Just married, I rode with other men to work.
We could've stood up in the bus's aisles
and undressed madly,
swapping pants and shirts and ties above traffic,
and stepped off afterwards
the same as we'd stepped on.

3

Now I slide into my shorts in the morning
and go about my day
like my children, as if skin were shelter enough.
Today the basket's weave is broken
so I hold the laundry damp and heavy against my chest,
take my time shaking out my children's shirts,
my wife's work dresses.
Later I will lift them, hot from the sun, off the line
and touch what will touch my family,
using my body to smooth and hold their clothes,
pressing their warmth into mine.

Too Late to Tell What Kind of Hawk It is

Let's go look at our bones,
my son says. And we find them where the creek elbows
into sand so clean we walk barefoot
to the bird's skull. Each day we inspect rot,
pry a little more flesh off the ribs.

We let the water do most of the peeling.
The feathers have been plucked already.
We may have already worn them in our hair.
Feathers have lives as absolute and separate from the body
as dreams. Water and wind bear them

to my son and me like dreams stolen off a corpse.
We wait for the skin to be washed away,
to be left only bones,
only longings. When I probe the ligaments,
I have to talk over my shoulder.

Some days I can't stop sniffing the decay
in my fingernails. I dig
under a wing. Between the pectorals.
My son picks up the skull with a stick.
I carry the talons.

When the creek is finally through with its dissection,
we will come back. We wait
for the water to scour all of the bones
old and holy
and then hand them to us to keep.

Parts of the Body

The loose skin of the elbow
when I hold my arm straight. Here I am animal
and old and tug
at the tough hide I've gathered around me.
Some places in the body
I touch as if they'd existed long before me
and I am wearing what's left of an earlier life.

I press down my lower lip and study it
in the mirror. I want to see
just how ugly I am inside,
how glistening, how durable.

The rich smell of the belly button.
I pull the stomach's skin away from its knot of flesh,
its five slits, and probe
with the sharp of my nail till I am afraid
I've gone too deep, I might
pierce the little privacy there, the knot's jealous secrets.

The hard skin by the nail
of the big toe,
place where I am indomitable and republican,
where the tough get going when the going gets tough.

The soft of my shoulder—
here I kiss
when I need to taste my own salt,
so I am sure of one thing,
this one thing.

Preen Glands

We swim till the waves flow from us,
then fold them under us like wings,
let them fan out from our flanks.
Daddy, we are angels.
Let's pretend we are angels.
Our plumage shifts, soft scapulars of foam,
the greater coverts,
the lesser coverts.

We follow the sweep of wings wide as the river,
lift the river when we rise.
Its surf sleeves our arms.
An angel must always feel such brilliance sliding from him,
a radiance heavy as the rapids.
To be raised by what bears us down,
brought high by a bright encumbrance of feathers.
Wings! my sons cry.

Daddy, look at my feathers.
See how the river fits.
We wear it all day.
Even I, their father, and beautiful.
Even my thirteen-year-old loves his body today.
How many quills cling to us,
what tiny follicles and white pith,
what webbing.

How hard an angel must concentrate
to hold such softness to him.

First Aid at 4 a.m.

In the one light on
in the house, he's gasping,
he's banging on the kitchen counter to call his family down
from sleep. He holds his throat,
sinks to his knees.
The cats circle around him, meowing,
waiting to be fed.
How odd it seems:
two weeks ago he nearly drove a car full of children into
another car. To die on the way to *Pinocchio*?
To choke to death on aspirin?
Then his thirteen-year-old's arms are reaching around him
from the back—they are astonishingly strong.
He feels the child's angry sobs
against his own weakening body,
the boy shouting, *Breathe, damn you,*
breathe, Daddy!
the boy half-saving his father,
half-hanging on.

Tape Recorder

In this modern age, we can die and still be heard,
our sons and daughters
touching the little window where our voices lie.

Tonight I go into my daughter's room
and gather her breathing,
next door place the microphone beside her brothers
and keep their dreams' slurred sentences.

When this was a new toy, all afternoon
the children held the mike to each other's mouths
for the silliness they'd play right back;
had they really said that,
were these voices how they actually sounded?

Once the boys hid the tape recorder under our bed
to hear the blankets being lifted off,
skin brushing skin,
so they might comprehend how life comes to be,
how they'd come to be.

When you are asleep, my inheritors,
I want to turn on the machine and sing softly into it,
to leave on the tape
a legacy, a song utterly personal.

But I can't.
These words are as far as I've dared to wander into song.
They are not what I wanted to leave.

From
STANDING WATCH

(Houghton Mifflin, 1978)

The Sitting

He would wake in the daybed to the scratching
of knife and thumbnail on canvas,
his mother erasing the skin off his face,
so she could raise the cheekbones
and darken the cheeks.
Her fingers smelled of linseed and turpentine.
They tipped his chin,
tightened around his jaw.
If no one else was there to model for her,
he'd have to do. He felt the skin slide over his jaws,
and he thought of the cat's skull
he had cupped in the woods like a bird's nest.
His mother made him sit for hours
while she rearranged his bones.
He tried not to move, to look as sadly beautiful
as the face she kept making vanish,
kept trying to work the light into,
to work light into her oils.
When he began finding her crying on curbstones,
he decided to be sick enough to stay home
and pose in the sunroom. He dozed off
listening to her press light into the canvas
till her brushes splayed, her knife failed her,
and he woke to find her painting with her fingers.
He was afraid to come home to alizarins
and cadmiums scrubbed off the handles of coffee cups,
burnt sienna removed from curtains, zinc white
from the dining-room table, another hired woman smiling
like a mother in a coloring book, the house
full of yellow flowers, everything faithful and copied.
Better to be home in the sunroom, sick
painter and model
and portrait, one white space left to be shadowed in,
his mother engaging daylight in conversation,
evening flattening his fleshtones as he tried not to move
out of the little light left her.

April 9, 1945/Bewahrung

From my house I was sure I could hear everything in the world.
I could tell the channel buoys
like the bells of different churches,
could hear the sea mumbling its low mass, hurrying the gospel,
mending the same dark clothing
it had been saving the poor for years.
I could hear each wave arrive late, slide into its pew;
tell each piece of change
dropping into the collection plate.

From my house I could hear everything—if I were quiet
I could tell between churches
like old boats in the harbor. I had closed my eyes so often
I knew whose hulls took the waves
like doors closing in empty factories, hulls of which fleet
rattled like windows shut all through a house.
I heard each church drift to tether's end
and pull at its slack—from my house I heard the churches creak
as they were tugged back.

From my house I could hear everything—if I did not move
I could hear everything else that did not move,
dark buildings groaning like wharves,
roofs I clung to
looking down, watching myself fall—I could tell the buildings
by how far they had sunk down,
which was Harvard, which Mother's hospital;
from my house I heard waves rise over its wards,
every day heard my mother drown.

From my house I was sure I heard everything else in the world,
all the countries shifting at their moorings.
Eyes closed, I could hear Germany move
among them like a freighter in too small a harbor.
I knew its cargo by its wake,
heard millions of small stones being scraped back.
From my house I heard the waves rise again
like bordering countries,
heard their feudal, cresting, holocaustal surf break.

Recess

Older boys drag younger by the wrists into woods,
children letting themselves go heavy,
letting themselves sink down inside their shirts.

My son backs against the walls
as if he were watching a brush fire spread towards him,
child by child; he looks away.

In half-empty subways I try not to gaze at coveys of thin boys
touching their hair as if on fire,
slicking down the flames.

Boys cursing, blowing smoke in our faces
as if they wanted us to rise
so they could set something else on fire.

As a child I knew I would always be afraid.
My son knows. I see it in his eyes,
in his soft, helpless hands after school.

I hear him in the white light before morning, in his terrible
and unsupervised recesses,
pressed to the wall, crying *uncle, uncle.*

Root Darkness

There was another darkness, the snake's
and the forsythia's: root darkness.
It was what flowed through their flat rakes,
what splashed their spades,
the high-water rim of the dark earth rising
and left for good on their shovel blades,
shadows left on stones that had been underground
longer than the boy had lived.
Darkness made him feel he had never lived,
as if he were a small possibility,
a word waiting to be spoken,
curled microfilm, a seed.

He felt like a seed in a seed's trance.
What would his father think of him, dreamy as clematis
floating off trellises? as seeds clinging
to each other like girls waiting to be asked to dance?
He crouched in the dark, earning his allowance,
wringing the necks of sheep sorrel
and chickweed, grasping for weeds
as if he were reaching into someone's throat
and drawing out the veins.
There was no darkness to his father, only a dusk
that smelled of wallets, smoking jackets, evening trains,
of light kept to a schedule.

He used to imagine his father could force the light
before its time, cut it back to the crown
of its roots, bury it outside.
It was his father who opened the windows,
sun leafing through the blinds
like chicory or endive through slats in a basket.
No one had ever died that the boy could remember;
his father kept everything alive.
Earth meant nothing to the boy but darkness.
What were their bodies but darkness,
pods of darkness that had not yet broken open?

His mother leaned over the porch rail, watching her garden
as if she had just set it down by the handle
so she could breathe in deep the bitter teas

of its turned-over peat moss. She liked to say
she was letting her garden steep.
She pressed his hands down into the earth
till he dared dig out new growth when he wrenched out old.
Your father hates to get his hands dirty.
She rubbed the boy's hands with soil, forced them
into the dirt. They weeded silently together,
left old roots to rot. The earth dried gray
on his fingers. In bed
he could still feel the dark earth rising to meet him.
The darkness was hers. He knew the darkness by her.

Adjust, Adjust

I was born committing suicide
holding my breath; they had to drag me kicking
out of that damp garage, airtight inside,
gases I struggled back to
until the doctor slapped me alive
and shouted, *Survive, survive.*

After Hiroshima, turning four,
I battered my head at the master bedroom door.
Every night I dreamt I was a child
burning at the town dump at the world's edge,
and every night my father yelled, *Be brave.*
Behave, behave.

I ripped his set of Plato at eight,
the year my mother was out, away at Boston State,
and war was fought in a darkness called Korea;
all winter I played dead in the corner
while my teachers clapped,
Adapt, adapt.

Grandmother took me in till I was ten;
with her silver carving knife, I locked her with me
in the den, all night clinging to her bathrobe, demanding
we cut our wrists in a lovers' pact.
The only answer I could secure
was *Endure, endure.*

I counted my bones waiting to be dead,
at thirteen an invalid in my nursing home, my bed,
watching Arkansas homemakers rail at Negro girls
between commercials, first graders
whom they tried to storm,
shrieking, *Nigger, nigger, conform.*

At fifteen, in South Station when I ran away every week,
I bedded down on papers ink-smudged with the blood
of freedom fighters, left in heaps in Hungary to decay,
while old men rubbed against my thighs,
lulling me to them with the hum,
Succumb, succumb.

Why couldn't I? When the world lapsed wide
and elastic into too much too-bright space when Kennedy died
and the road wore bald and the yards stretched
between houses, the towns gleamed like chrome, I drove
into walls, day after day,
and the police shrugged like uncles. *Obey, obey.*

Can't you bleed? Coward, can't you die
while wrists are cut, throats slit, children gassed
in Vietnam? At twenty-four can you only cry
while men shoot themselves to death in the DMZ?
Your analyst coughs, *You must, Christopher,*
adjust, adjust.

Other Rooms

In most houses there is a room a child will not enter,
a drawer he will not pull out
when anyone is home. Every child has one old woman
whose kisses he cannot forget.
Every boy has a place between home and somewhere else,
sag in a fence, dry belly of a puddle,
curbstone where he widens cracks others have opened.
Every boy has one street he looks for
from a train or bus window and wonders
what it would be like to buy a soda in that small corner store,
to sip it on the high stone steps
of the row house and watch the train
leave. Every boy has a place where he wishes he'd said *yes*,
a city street just late enough to make someone else
look older, a guest cottage,
a friend of his father's, a waiting room,
a place he looks for afterward,
its padded old men scrimmaging, practicing blocks,
pants slipping off them like hip pads, voices slurred
as if through mouth guards
as they mumble scores of games or names of girls,
secret places where they hid
as children, lean over him, runaway fathers
puzzling out the new math
of his body. Every boy has one man he remembers
who touched him till he felt himself
tilting as if trying to stand in a small boat,
one young man who spoke German
and whose fingernails smelled of smoke.
Always one room he's sorry he never entered.

Dictionary Johnson

*I saw that one enquiry only gave occasion to another, that book
referred to book, that to search was not always to find, and to find
was not always to be informed; and thus to pursue perfection was,
like the first inhabitants of Arcadia, to chase the sun, which, when
they had reached the hill where he seemed to rest, was still beheld
at the same distance from them.*
—S. Johnson "Preface to the Dictionary"

House to market, church
to tavern, the man whose job it was to decide
what went into the dictionary,
and what did not, counted the steps. He made sure
his foot touched a particular stone at a particular time
and turned back if his fingers failed to brush every post
along the way. No walk
for the great man was ever simple. No floor
safe till he tried its strength,

no sentence. It helped to know
that someone I was studying in school,
a man who held himself responsible
for the entire English language,
was as screwed up as I was. In the midst of decisions
I was convinced at eighteen
would determine the rest of my life—whether or not
to quit the football team or smile
at a certain boy or girl or take Calculus I or Spanish IV—
it was comforting to think of Dr. Johnson,

standing at the top of the hill of a great estate
and slowly removing from his pockets
keys, watch, purse,
and handing them all to the lord of the manor
and then falling upon the grass
and rolling down, down, down
like a great boulder that would not be stopped
till he hit the bottom,
and then rising and with as much dignity
as when he'd greeted the king, going back up the slope
and flinging his body back down
as if there was real pleasure in doing certain things
over and over and it took a great man
to know what they were.

Acknowledgments

Thanks to generous editors, judges, readers, teachers, poets: X. J. Kennedy, Janine Cole, Jonathan Galassi, Maria Mazziotti-Gillan, James Freeman, Ted and Renee Weiss, Robert Fink, Betsy Sholl, George Drew, Joan Aleshire, Jonathan Holden, Helen Lawton Wilson, Steven Riel, Pam Perkins-Frederick, Elizabeth Raby, Patricia Goodrich, Bev Stoughton, Ellen Bryant Voigt, Sandra Becker, Alicia Ostriker, Lucille Clifton, Pam Bernard, Steven Huff, April Ossmann, Sy Safransky, Andrew Snee, Phil Fried, Judith Kitchen, Ellen Bryant Voigt, Sandy Solomon, Julie Bruck, Rona Cohen, Anne Tax, Peter Bridge, Cornelius Eady, Robert Fishman, Jack Bursk, Deda Kavanagh, Rosemary O'Keefe, Robert Fraser, Lynn Levin, Lorraine Henri Lins, Wendy Fulton Steginsky, Katherine Falk, Camille Norvaissas, Diana Weiss, Christine McKee, Marie Kane, Hayden Saunier, Teresa Mendez Quigley, Luray Gross, Carolina Morales, and all the brave and inspiring Spring Workshop poets.

Thanks also to the magazines in which some of these poems appeared: *Another Chicago Magazine, Bellingham Review, Beloit Poetry Journal, Bucks County Writer, College English, Images, Manhattan Review, New England Review, New Letters, North American Review, Poetry, Poetry Now, The Sun.*

"The Visitor," "What If You Could Be Any Letter," "Multiple Personality Disorder," "F," "Ode to J," "Letter L," "Babbadino," "At an Early Age," "The Pathetic Fallacy," "Say the Magic Word," "What's Missing in the Dictionary," "Dictionary Johnson" are from Christopher Bursk's *The First Inhabitants of Arcadia,* copyright 2006. Reproduced by permission of University of Arkansas Press.

"The Soul Wants the Last Word," "Why I Hate Math," "August 6," "Singing Yourself Down the Stairs," "Utopia," "College Professor Suspended," "E Pluribus Unum," "42 Linden," "De Rerum Natura," are from Christopher Bursk's *The Improbable Swervings of Atoms,* copyright 2005. Reprinted by permission of University of Pittsburgh Press.

"Ovid at Fifteen," "Rorschach Test," "Ovid, Book Three," "Teaching the Myth of Pelops," "Why You Find So Many A's on my Class Roster," "Big Nose Relegated," "O Beauty, Fugitive Beauty," "The Suicide Note," "Aristaeus" are from Christopher Bursk's *Ovid at Fifteen,* copyright 2003. Reprinted by permission of New Issues, Western Michigan University.

"Ovid at Fifteen," "Rorschach Test," "Ovid, Book Three," are from Christopher Bursk's *Working the Stacks,* copyright 2002. Reprinted by permission of Bacchae Press.

Cover art by Justin Bursk; author photo by Christine Mydlo; cover and interior book design by Diane Kistner (dkistner@futurecycle.org); Gentium Book Basic text with Cronos Pro titling

∞

About FutureCycle Press

FutureCycle Press is dedicated to publishing lasting English-language poetry books, chapbooks, and anthologies in both print-on-demand and ebook formats. Founded in 2007 by long-time independent editor/publishers and partners Diane Kistner and Robert S. King, the press incorporated as a nonprofit in 2012. A number of our editors are distinguished poets and writers in their own right, and we have been actively involved in the small press movement going back to the early seventies.

The FutureCycle Poetry Book Prize and honorarium is awarded annually for the best full-length volume of poetry we publish in a calendar year. Introduced in 2013, our Good Works projects are anthologies devoted to issues of universal significance, with all proceeds donated to a related worthy cause. Our Selected Poems series highlights contemporary poets with a substantial body of work to their credit; with this series we strive to resurrect work that has had limited distribution and is now out of print.

We are dedicated to giving all of the authors we publish the care their work deserves, making our catalog of titles the most diverse and distinguished it can be, and paying forward any earnings to fund more great books.

We've learned a few things about independent publishing over the years. We've also evolved a unique, resilient publishing model that allows us to focus mainly on vetting and preserving for posterity the most books of exceptional quality without becoming overwhelmed with bookkeeping and mailing, fundraising activities, or taxing editorial and production "bubbles." Come see what we're doing at www.futurecycle.org.

The FutureCycle Poetry Book Prize

All full-length volumes of poetry published by FutureCycle Press in a given calendar year are considered for the annual FutureCycle Poetry Book Prize. This allows us to consider each submission on its own merits, outside of the context of a contest. Too, the judges see the finished book, which will have benefitted from the beautiful book design and strong editorial gloss we are famous for.

The book ranked the best in judging is announced as the prize-winner in the subsequent year. There is no fixed monetary award; instead, the winning poet receives an honorarium of 20% of the total net royalties from all poetry books and chapbooks the press sold online in the year the winning book was published. The winner is also accorded the honor of being on the panel of judges for the next year's competition and, in this capacity, receives a copy of all books in contention for that year's prize.

* 9 7 8 1 9 3 8 8 5 3 5 1 7 *